THE
AMERICAN
PRIVATEERS

THE

AMERICAN

PRIVATEERS

By Donald Barr Chidsey

ILLUSTRATED

DODD, MEAD & COMPANY
NEW YORK
1962

☆ CONTENTS

☆ ILLUSTRATIONS

Following page 86

Illustrations courtesy of Peabody Museum, Salem, Massachusetts

THE
AMERICAN
PRIVATEERS

1 ☆ THE FIGHT AT FAYAL

When the schooner *General Armstrong* dropped her anchor at Fayal, the Azores, the afternoon of September 26, 1814, all she was looking for was drinking water. She never did get it. She got immortality instead.

General Armstrong was a privateer, and she had done more than her share of fighting in this second war with Great Britain. She carried a rather unusual armament for a privateer—a 24-pound long gun mounted on a swivel amidships and three 9-pounders on either side. Her crew numbered 90.

Captain Samuel Chester Reid was thirty-one. He had been at sea since he was eleven, much of that time in the regular Navy, and he knew his business. He hailed from Norwich, Connecticut.

General Armstrong herself hailed from New York, and was named after a distinguished New Yorker, John Armstrong, a former Secretary of War. She'd had a hard time, on this cruise, getting *out* of New York, so determined was the British blockade off Sandy Hook. She had been chased by a frigate and a ship of the line, but had outpaced both.

She had taken a small brig, *Perry*, but released her when she turned out to be another American privateer. *Perry* had thrown all her guns overboard to lighten herself when chased by a British frigate the previous day, and now she was on her way back to Philadelphia to get some more armament.

In mid-Atlantic *General Armstrong* had come upon a British ship of the line, a towering giant that could have blasted her out of the water in any kind of stand-up fight. *Armstrong* had exchanged a few shots with her at long distance, out of sheer good spirits, before running away. This was a common practice among Yankee privateering skippers toward the end of the War of 1812. They knew how violently the British naval officers hated them and their kind, and it pleased the privateers to taunt them.

And now the schooner was here in Fayal, where there wasn't a breath of breeze, and sunset was near.

Captain Reid went ashore and looked up the United States consul, John B. Dabney, who said certainly, he could arrange to get some drinking water for the schooner.

They were interrupted by a lookout's shout announcing a sail, which was just outside of the harbor to the northeast and which had signalled for a pilot.

She was British, that was sure. She was brig-rigged and pierced for many cannons. (She proved in fact to be *Carnation*, 18 guns, and her skipper, Lloyd, was even more rancorous toward American privateers than were most of his kind.)

"I can't move, except with sweeps, and that would carry me right past her," said Captain Reid. "Will she let us alone, d'ye think?"

"She'll have to," said Consul Dabney. "After all, this is a neutral harbor."

"Yes, but still. . . ."

Reid went back aboard. He knew that Fayal was a neutral harbor, but he also knew something about British naval officers, those arrogant men, and he wasn't taking any chances.

There was still some air just outside the harbor, and *Carnation*, in contrast to the beehive-like activity of her seamen as witnessed from afar, drifted languidly in.

Reid upped anchor and with the aid of sweeps, or long oars, posted his craft much closer to the shore, as close as he dared, right under the guns of the castle. There he anchored again, fore and aft, but he put springs on his cables so that he could make a dash for it if a breeze should spring up.

The British brig could not reach him there. She drew too much water. He could see that at a glance. But she did keep getting nearer.

In the tawny sunset—there wasn't a cloud in the sky and the moon was scheduled to rise early and to be almost full—two other vessels were seen approaching the harbor from the northeast. They were British war vessels all right, as Reid's glass told him. (They proved to be the 74-gun frigate *Plantagenet* and the brig-of-war *Rota*, 38 guns.) Like *Carnation*, they were carrying troops to Jamaica, in the West Indies, where Major General Sir Edward Pakenham was assembling forces for a tremendous attack on New Orleans. Also like *Carnation*, and like *General Armstrong* too, they had come to Fayal looking not for trouble, but for drinking water.

Reid ordered his men and boys to battle stations. They knew their business. *Armstrong* did not have an inch of canvas spread, so there was no need to worry about running gear or to man the helm. Every gunner, every layer, every powder monkey was at his post. Tubbed matches were lit. Sand was spread on deck. Swabs, wormers, linstocks, rammers, ball racks, bags of grape, all were set out in their proper places. Boarding nets were spread clear around the schooner—not past the shrouds, as would have been done if a boarding party was expected directly from another vessel, but below the gunnels outside; for if the British boarded at all it would have to be from small boats.

Then there was nothing to do but wait.

Word had got out in the town behind them that a battle might be making up in the bay, and there was a great deal of scurrying back and forth and jockeying for positions. The shore indeed was black with men, all holding their breaths. The Governor himself was on hand, in an advantageous position in a tower of the fort.

The guns of that fort had been run out, and they bristled menacingly; but Reid knew—for Dabney had told him—that most of those guns were mere show pieces, antiques that would never be fired again, even if there had been powder and shot. Besides, Portugal would not resist with force an invasion by the British Navy, no matter how flagrant a violation of international law it might be. Reid could not count on any support there.

At eight o'clock four boats put out from *Carnation*, which was now anchored near at hand, as close as she dared to come.

These were large, long boats of the barge type, just the

kind that would be used in a board or a cutting-out operation. There might have been thirty men in each, and the men were all armed.

The moon was just about to rise. In a few minutes the whole bay would be bathed in its light. Everybody aboard *General Armstrong* could see that the Britishers were hoping to take them by surprise, while it still was dark.

Pikes and cutlasses, muskets, daggers, and pistols, were passed out. The gunners blew on their matches, from which columns of smoke wobbled.

Captain Reid cupped his hands and hailed the boats. What did they want?

They stopped, close together, huddled, the officers no doubt dismayed to learn that they had been seen.

There was a pause, and Reid called again.

Then the Britishers broke into action, no longer trying to keep quiet, their rowers putting full backs into it, their marines cocking muskets.

"*Fire!*" cried Captain Reid.

It was all over in a few minutes. Some of the Britishers fired back, and a few even found marks—the first mate of *General Armstrong* was wounded in the shoulder and a seaman was killed—but when the small boats paused, shocked, the long toms let them have it again, and that was the end of that; they scampered in retreat.

The gunners swabbed their pieces, and the monkeys brought up extra powder.

For there would be more. Everybody knew that there would be more. Englishmen don't give up that easily.

Ashore, Consul Dabney hurried to the Governor and demanded that he protest against this gross violation of neutrality. The Governor agreed, and he sat down and penned a stiff note to Captain Lloyd, who was brusque, being much too busy to bother about rights of neutrality— or any other kind.

By this time the moon was fully up, and those aboard of *General Armstrong* could see that all three war vessels were frantically signalling to one another, though what they said the Americans did not know, for of course a code was used. (This then was called, in Navy parlance, "a telegraph," which of course is exactly what it was; for many years after Samuel Morse made known his invention, *it* used to be called an *electric* telegraph.)

They not only signalled: they sent boats back and forth. Clearly the captains were conferring, and it was obvious too that another and much larger boarding party was being organized.

This work was done fast. It was only about nine o'clock when twenty-odd boats put out from behind *Carnation*. There must have been four hundred men in them.

Some of the boats had carronades mounted in the bow. Short, snub-nosed cannons, named after the Carron Iron Foundry on the Carron River, Sterlingshire, Scotland, these could be devastating at a short distance.

Yet it was evident to the Americans that the organization was not yet complete, for the boats did not attack immediately. Instead they took refuge behind a rocky reef, and stayed there for some time to re-equip and rearrange themselves and to get final orders.

It was close to midnight when at last they sallied forth.

They came very fast, in two divisions, one heading for

the bow of *General Armstrong,* the other for the stern, where Captain Reid himself was in charge.

This battle was a real one, and lasted about forty minutes. Again and again the British tried to board, and again and again they were beaten back. All of the fighting was with small arms; the long toms could no longer be brought to bear.

The slaughter among the English was appalling. Their boats floated free, filled with the dead and dying. Many men panicked and jumped overboard to swim to shore, so that the stretch between *General Armstrong* and the beach below the castle was stippled with bobbing heads.

Second Mate Alexander O. Williams dropped dead, a musket ball smack in the middle of his forehead. The first mate had been knocked out of action in the original brush, and now, forward, the third mate fell with a shattered leg. The fight there wavered.

Captain Reid saw this, or sensed it. The stern, where he commanded in person, was clear of small boats now. They'd had enough, back there. But men were scrabbling up the sides of the forecastle with renewed vigor.

Reid rallied his lads and led them all forward.

That was the break of the battle. Flesh and blood could stand no more. The British fell back.

Reid had lost two dead, seven wounded. The British, by their own admission—Reid always contended that the real figure was much greater—had 63 killed, 110 wounded.

Next morning Captain Lloyd of *Carnation* opened up with his guns on *General Armstrong.* He had more than twice as many guns as the Yankees, and in addition *Rota* and *Plantagenet* were now in position to open up.

A few shots went beyond *General Armstrong* and into the town, where a woman suffered a shattered thigh and a boy and much livestock were killed; but at that distance most of them, understandably, hulled the schooner.

Reid did the proper thing. Outnumbered and outgunned ten to one, he nailed his colors to the mast, buried his dead, sent his wounded ashore, threw all of his guns and all his powder overboard, and then scuttled the schooner so that she sank to the bottom—which was not far. After that, taking his time, he saw to it that every one of his men got safely ashore, himself the last of all.

Soon afterward the British boarded *General Armstrong* unopposed, and they burned her.

However, even ashore, in Portuguese territory, the Americans were not safe. The British landed not only burying parties but also press gangs, claiming that two of the Americans were deserters from the British Navy.

Reid led his men back into the hills, where they commandeered a monastery and placed it into a posture of defense. The British came, took a look, and decided not to attack.

However, caring for their wounded—a couple of sloops of war, *Thais* and *Calypso*, came along just then and were used as hospital ships—repairing their boats, and burying their dead took up so much of the Britishers' time it was October 4, more than a week later, before they continued their voyage toward Jamaica.

That week held up General Pakenham's plans for the

attack on New Orleans. And it may have made all the difference in that crucial campaign, for Andrew Jackson was desperately pressed for time.

General Armstrong had not died in vain.

2 ☆ NOT TO SPLIT HAIRS

Why did so many people hate privateering? What was there about this old-time profession that made otherwise sane sailors—landsmen as well—see red?

First, some definitions. It is important that you know, right off, what privateering was—and wasn't.

It was once a widely practiced institution in America; it was a way of life; but it has been dead for more than a hundred years now, and present-day ideas of what it was are likely to be blurred and faint.

Privateering was private war, at sea.

Once it had been private war on land as well. In the old days when a man had been offended by somebody across a border, and his chief or king or feudal lord did not wish to have a full-fledged, formal war on his hands, but sympathized with the man, a letter of marque might be issued giving that man permission to raise an army at his own expense and to cross the border at his own risk and to get back what he thought he was rightfully entitled to—if he could. That sounds mad to us today: it would set the whole world on fire. It seemed perfectly simple then, and even natural.

When wars were not so appallingly expensive and destructive there were more of them, and they could be entrusted to private parties.

The first letters of marque, or privateering licenses, then, were retaliatory measures—or at least pretended to be.

It soon became clear that private war on land was not practical. It led to many embarrassing situations. It provoked too many reprisals. Besides, it was generally agreed, private property, unless it was out-and-out munitions of war, should be held inviolable, untouchable. To be sure, as long as there were soldiers there would be looting, but it must be *unofficial* looting, punishable, frowned upon; for ordinary purposes an army would pay for whatever it thought it had to take.

This accepted principle applied only to land war. On the high seas—that is, outside the three-mile limit, a limit agreed upon because at that time three miles was about as far as the best cannon could carry—all rules were off.

The theory was that since the sea belonged to nobody it belonged to everybody, and since it was not ruled by any acknowledged state or sovereign power it had no laws at all. When there was a war going on, as there usually was, private property that was three miles or more out had nothing sacred about it. It was free game. It could be *legally* seized.

Privateers took not just lead and gunpowder, bayonets and military boots—though they took these whenever they got a chance—but in a much greater degree they took lard, molasses, lumber, dried fish, salt, and anything else they considered marketable.

What was the difference between privateering and piracy? The difference is simple, but very important.

Piracy was *illegal* stealing at sea—or on land after a descent from the sea. That was the crime: theft. Assault, insult, mayhem, and murder might be parts of the piracy, but they were not essential parts.

The privateer had his paper, his license. The pirate had none. The privateer was allowed to plunder the ships of a given foreign nation only when his own nation was at war with that nation, and even then there were restrictions as to time and, often, territory. The license might be good for a year, six months, or even only three months, and sometimes it could not be used south or east or west or north of certain lines of latitude and longitude.

And often in the earlier days of privateering only certain types of cargo were made subject to stealing. But in the golden age—the War of 1812—the privateer could take everything aboard an enemy vessel, besides taking the vessel itself.

In one of those word-association tests so popular today, suppose that you were given "pirate." It is ten to one that you would respond with "buried treasure." There was nothing like that in connection with privateering. In the first place, privateers seldom got a chance to lift church plate, silks of Samarkand, pearls, rubies from Mogok, and great brassbound chests filled with Spanish eight-real pieces (Long John Silver's parrot's "pieces-of-eight"). In the second place, whatever they took was not legally theirs until it had been brought to one of their own ports where there was a vice-admiralty court. Then it was libelled (*officially* seized) and condemned and finally awarded to them. After that, it still had to be sold. So why bury it?

The pirate, on the other hand, was a law unto himself, or tried to be. He was a thief in times of peace as well as in times of war, robbing from vessels of any nationality, without respect for lines of latitude or longitude or for limits of time. The pirate was an outlaw, an enemy of all the human race. Every man's hand should be raised against him. And helping a pirate was in itself a punishable offense. The pirate had declared war upon his own kind, so there was only one punishment for him—death. In every land and at every time the whole weight of the law was against piracy.

Now, it is true that privateers not infrequently lapsed; they "went on the account" and became pirates. But the distinction is still there, as it was there three hundred years ago.

Some other names:

Corsair is simply the French for "courser," one who hunts down game. It was applied to privateers and pirates alike, though in English a "courser" or one who coursed or who was "on the course" could only be a pirate. And it generally meant that in French, too.

A *rover* might or might not have been a pirate in fact, but he was probably a pirate at heart. It was a rather poetical designation, and never had anything to do with privateering, which was not a bit poetical.

Freebooter came from the Dutch word *vrijbuiter*, which

might be translated as "free-booty-er." It meant a pirate, undoubtedly.

Filibuster was a corruption of "freebooter," probably by way of the Spanish *filibustero* or the French *filibustier*. The latter spelling indeed was common in English until the middle of the nineteenth century, when the word took on a new meaning as well as a new spelling, unaccountably coming to stand for a *nordamericano* soldier of fortune who operated in South or Central America—a man like William Walker, who was called the "King of the Filibusters." Later still, in the twentieth century, it meant a legal but objectionable trick for obstructing the passage of legislation, usually by talking it to death.

Buccaneer is in another class entirely. The buccaneers originally and properly were men who hunted, slaughtered, and roasted or smoked the wild oxen and cattle with which some of the West Indian islands had been stocked years before—by pirates, likely enough, since pirates, denied the standard ports, were always looking for something to eat. The buccaneers sold this meat to the crews of passing vessels, who, again, could have been and often were pirates. The buccaneers did their roasting on wooden frames which were called *buccans* (today we call them barbecues); hence the name. They were a rough, wild lot, the buccaneers, and though few of them were sailing men they often volunteered for piratical descents upon nearby shores. Henry Morgan's men at Panama were largely buccaneers, in the then accepted meaning of the word.

Not every buccaneer was a part-time pirate, though many were, and probably very few full-time pirates ever had been buccaneers. The names, however, became mixed

in the public imagination until they grew to be synony-
mous—at least in the Caribbean area.

Now let's take a few examples.

Sir Francis Drake was a privateer, not a pirate. Undoubtedly he had Queen Elizabeth's permission for what
he did. Although he never did produce this permission and
it may have been merely verbal, Drake was at least semi-
official. He was never an outlaw. A preacher's son and very
devout, he justified his depredations by explaining that the
Spaniards had set upon and robbed him at San Juan de
Ulna (the present Veracruz, Mexico). Now he was only
getting his own back—at the point of a gun, to be sure, and
with something like 10,000 per cent interest. However he
could never afford to slip; for if he failed the Queen might
disown him or even cut off his head. But Drake didn't
mind that. He was used to taking chances.

John Paul Jones, in the eyes of the British, was a pirate.
They called him that often, and vehemently. But in American eyes he was not even a privateer, for he held a captain's commission in the United States Navy. Yet the
British, who did not recognize the United States Navy,
probably would have hanged him if they'd caught him.
They did not catch him.

The so-called Sallee pirates and the Barbary Coast pirates of Africa were in truth privateers, though from the
Western point of view they were particularly obnoxious
privateers. They had bases. They had licenses. They even
had a legal excuse for what they did. We know today that
their activities were in truth a form of international blackmail; still they must be classed as privateers, not pirates.

On the other hand, the brothers Lafitte, Pierre and Jean, have been called inaccurately "the last of the pirates," but only because they were not the last. The practice of piracy persisted until very recent times along the China coast. The Lafittes were certainly pirates. They protested that they were privateers, because they only stole, on the high seas anyway, from Spanish vessels, and they held or claimed to hold a commission for the Republic of Cartagena in South America authorizing them to do just that. However at that time the Republic of Cartagena was purely a paper affair, a fiction. Queen Elizabeth I, the Emperor of Morocco, the Dey of Algiers and others of his ilk, not to mention the infant United States of America, were sovereigns or states recognized by at least some of their sovereign neighbors. The Republic of Cartagena was to be sure at war with Spain at that time, but nobody *recognized* Cartagena as a republic—nobody, that is, except the brothers Lafitte. Yes, they were pirates.

3 ☆ PEACE MAKES PIRATES

The people of colonial America were a maritime people. They thought in terms of the sea, which so recently they or their parents had crossed. They were not yet ready to challenge the land behind them, that dark savage place, and they had carved for themselves only a thin strip of coastline. None of them ever lived far from the sound of breakers.

The Atlantic was life. It was Home. Before you could gather your strength for an assault upon the wilderness you must face and deal with the Atlantic.

Just about every "boughten" thing that the American colonists owned, as distinguished from the many things they made, came to them by way of the sea—all their metal, all their tools, their weapons.

These colonists, too, were largely dependent upon fish, which meant more sailing. In the absence of roads, trade with one another was carried on by coastal boats they themselves had made. Salt water, you might say, was soaked into their very furniture.

One product they did have, and in plenty: they had wood. The forests, growing right down to the waterline, seemed to be inexhaustible. Many of the articles that among a people less poor would be made of metal, in colonial America were made of wood—dinner plates, spoons, hay forks, nails. The nails, pencil-like pins, were called "treenails," which was pronounced and sometimes spelled "trunnels." You can still find them in old houses or old boats.

It was no more than natural, then, that shipbuilding came to be one of their chief industries. At first the vessels were made for the colonists' own use, and were small; but soon many an English merchant learned that he could get the same ship built in America for only a little more than one third of its cost in an English shipyard, and he acted accordingly.

This was not because labor was cheaper in America;

indeed, it was better paid than in England. It was because the British forests had been so thinned over the years and were situated so far back from the shore that heavy restrictions were placed on the cutting of trees. So carrying timber to the shipyards was an expensive business—much of it in fact had to be imported from Sweden. In the American colonies, however, great stands of oak, cedar, hickory, and ash reached right down to the beach.

Fittings had to be fetched from across the sea, true. Iron mines, if there was any iron in this New World, decidedly were *not* near the sea; and so, at first, they were not even sought. There was another reason as well. The colonial policy of England, like that of other European nations, decreed that colonies should be mere feeders of the Mother Country and should never be allowed any trade of their own, much less industry. The government at London would have looked with heavy disapproval on any attempt to set up an American smelter or iron foundry. However, very little metal went into a merchant ship of those days anyway.

Then again, if the vessel was destined for a West Indian run and should have her bottom sheathed against the teredos worm, the job could be done in England, after her first crossing. The colonies were not allowed sheet metal of any kind.

The colonies did have hemp for the manufacture of rope, a manufacture that they were graciously permitted, and their rope-walks were many, some of them more than five hundred yards long.

This building of boats was not confined to the cities. The average man who had need of any manner of boat would no more think of hiring somebody to make it for him than he would think of hiring somebody to shave his face. He'd do it himself, of course. If he didn't have the tools he would make them, or borrow them. If he did not have a saw pit he would dig one. As for the scaffolding and the launching ways, these could be thrown up for the occasion —using wood, of course.

The "amphibious farmers," whose property fringed the very shore itself, fished by custom in season, using boats that they themselves had built in their spare time, just as they had built the houses in which they lived. They took all this for granted.

When they built seagoing ships to order, the Americans were conventional enough, at least at first; but when they built smaller vessels they displayed great originality of design, favoring a shallow draft for rivers and bays, favoring too the fore-and-aft rig over the clumsy square that European builders clung to. Thus the schooner was developed here.

The schooner, surely, was one of the most *telling* vessels in maritime history. It changed the course of events, time after time. Yet nobody knows who invented it, if indeed any one man did. But it was certainly American. Its inspiration was here.

American vessels, though small, were fast. This point is important. Speed counted for a great deal with smugglers, which many Americans became when Great Britain began to impose oppressive trade regulations on her colonies. Speed counted for a great deal, too, with privateers. They needed speed just as a swordsman needs a long arm and long legs. A man who attacks should be equipped to attack fast, and a man who runs away should run fast.

When the chance came, the colonists were ready.

In this they were encouraged by the Home government in England, which was glad to get any help against its enemies, and which managed to stay more or less embroiled in war for most of the latter part of the seventeenth century and just about all of the eighteenth.

To the American colonists these wars were lucrative.

After the troubled period of the Protectorate, 1653–1658, there was peace for a little while. And then there was the Dutch War of 1672–1674.

At first the colonists played little part in this Dutch War, for two reasons. The Dutch did not then have any considerable possessions in the West Indies; and the West Indies, taken as a whole, were considered the richest territory, the finest prize, in the world, and were especially attractive to the hungry colonists of mainland North America.

Also, the Dutch were firmly settled at Nieuw Amsterdam, were prodigious shipbuilders in their own right, and were sometimes short-tempered, aggressive. A touch of privateering might cause the Dutch to send a fleet against the unprotected shores of New Jersey, Connecticut, Rhode Island, or Massachusetts.

However, once Nieuw Amsterdam had been taken by an English fleet, and the name changed to New York in honor of the King's brother, the colonists soon fitted out a swarm of small, fast, effective vessels, one of the biggest investors being the Governor of Rhode Island, Benedict Arnold, great-grandfather of the traitor.

So long as Charles II and James II were on the throne of England and Scotland there was not likely to be a war with France, no matter what the provocation, for these Stuarts owed a huge debt, both financial and spiritual, to France. When James fled, however, and that dour Dutchman, William of Orange, came over to rule the island, things were different.

William hated France, and very soon he took his new holding into war with her, a war (1689–1697) that was appropriately named after him—King William's War.

It was then that privateering really began to blossom in the American colonies.

When William died there was peace, but everybody knew that it would not last long. Nor did it. In 1702 there broke out a renewal of the conflict that was to last for eleven years. This is known, formally, as the War of the Spanish Succession, though in America at the time it was generally called Queen Anne's War.

Then there was a war with Spain, 1739–1748, popularly dubbed the War of Jenkin's Ear. The American colonists made a good thing out of this, too. The colonists liked wars—in Europe. Your home was safe, and you could make money out of privateering.

The War of the Austrian Succession (in America, King George's War) lasted from 1740 to 1748, though once again when it was ended everybody knew that here was no more than a truce, that France and Great Britain (it was Great Britain now, for England and Scotland had united) still had plenty to fight about.

In connection with this war the British Parliament passed several pieces of legislation designed to encourage legitimate and to discourage illegitimate privateering. The chief of these was 32 George II, 25: "An Act for the Encouragement of Seamen and the Prevention of Piracies by Private Ships of War." This provided, among other things, that only a vessel of at least ten guns, 3-pounders or bigger, could be licensed for privateering. This was meant to quash the "shore pirates," who at night in open boats would row out to anchored vessels and swarm over them. These gentry were in no position actually to take over these vessels, they were intent only upon an immediate cash ransom. 32 George II, 25 specifically forbade such ransoming, which, however, was not often imposed off American shores. This was an effort, and a sound one, to make privateering a somewhat more responsible, even respectable business.

Finally there was the Seven Years War (the French and Indian War in American history books), which really did decide the issue, for a while anyway.

The winner, Great Britain, triumphantly took over all of Canada. In this war the American colonists had been used in other ways than privateering, though there was God's plenty of that too. For the first time, Great Britain demanded help—and got it. The colonists did their share in the conquest of Canada, and afterward were to wish that they hadn't.

From this time on, the War of the American Revolution was inevitable. Great Britain, badly crippled, almost bankrupt, resented the colonies' ambition to make some of their own goods, and she imposed the intolerable Regulatory Trade Acts. Also, Great Britain thought that the colonies should pay for the upkeep of the troops stationed among them for their own good (as she put it), and she taxed accordingly. These actions raised a howl of protest on this side of the Atlantic.

It seems odd that the one thing parent and child had done together, the winning of Canada, should cause them at last to separate so bloodily; but that's the way the world was.

Now, it might be thought that when war was over a privateer would be glad to go home and get down to the pestiferous paperwork involved in collecting his prize money, if any, especially since he could be sure that there would be another war along in a little while. This was often the case. But at other times it was not the case.

Except for the bookkeeping, privateering, while admittedly perilous, was easy. Men got used to it. They failed to see why they should return to real labor on land. They had all the equipment, they had the experience, and there would be more merchant vessels than ever, so why should they start for home just because their privateering commissions had expired with the peace?

Some did not. They went "on the account." They cut their ties with civilization.

There was a saying at the time that "peace makes pirates."

Which brings us to the curious case of Captain Kidd.

4 ☆ YOU CAN'T EAT DIAMONDS

William Kidd was a stolid, substantial citizen, a Scot by birth, a minister's son, who had spent most of his life at sea. True, he tended to drink too much at times, and his temper was said to be touchy. On the whole, however, he was thought safe and sound, eminently respectable. He owned his own house in New York, where he had settled down to trade, and he owned other houses there too, for he had invested in real estate. He was married to a well-thought-of churchgoer, and they had a son. In 1693 when William Kidd made a business trip to London, in his own sloop, he was nearing fifty, a grave, earnest man.

True, he had been a privateer, but who in that seagoing community hadn't? His record was clean, even meritorious. The pitch of piracy had never smutted him.

In the British capital he encountered an old acquaintance, Robert Livingston of the famous New York family, who introduced him to the Earl of Bellomont. This nobleman had just been appointed governor of the Massachusetts Bay Colony, which at that time included practically all of what is now New England. One of the instructions

Bellomont had received with his appointment was to do something about the pirates, who were becoming increasingly bold everywhere in the world. He was looking for a man who could help him in this—a man who might also, at the same time, show a profit. He had in mind a private venture, a private crusade, appropriately financed.

Colonel Livingston recommended William Kidd, and it was so decided. They drew up an agreement. They formed a company.

Lord Bellomont let a few friends in on what looked to be a good thing—Lord Orford, Lord Somers, Lord Romney, and the Duke of Shrewsbury, all of them in the government, in the Cabinet. Today this would be highly unethical, if not illegal. It was natural then. There was nothing sinister about it.

King William himself issued the privateering commission to "our beloved friend William Kidd." That much was easy, since Somers was the Lord Chancellor of England, Orford was First Lord of the Admiralty, and Romney was a secretary of state.

The government itself would put no money into the enterprise, of course. This would all be done privately, as the practice had been for many years. It was to be on a "no purchase (plunder), no pay" basis. Kidd, who with Colonel Livingston had taken a fifth share in the business, was perfectly satisfied with that provision.

He was expected to catch pirates. That indeed was his assignment.

He went back to New York, where he purchased and equipped the *Adventure Galley*, 287 tons, 34 guns, 154 men. He sailed in September of 1696.

It is significant that he made straight for St. Mary's.

St. Mary's is a very small island about ten miles east of the northern part of the very large island of Madagascar, in the Indian Ocean just off Africa. St. Mary's is about sixty miles long and about ten miles across, and in the seventeenth century it was largely jungle, its principal products being cattle, slaves, and pirates.

Here the rovers got their supplies and hoarded their loot. Here they held their share-outs. And it was here too that in retirement or semi-retirement, surrounded by slaves and colorful concubines, they built for themselves castles—of wood, to be sure, but featuring turrets and moats and all the rest of it—and called themselves kings.

They were sometimes referred to as the Red Sea Men, but they also operated in the Persian Gulf and along the Malabar Coast, where the pickings were good. In that lush land, that land of fresh fruit, good water, and good firewood too, they were right in the southeast trade winds, and until they had made the place notorious they could hope for many visits from passing mariners, *friskable* mariners.

They had nothing to fear from the natives, who were broken into many warring factions. Indeed this helped, for with their modern weapons they could join one side or the other, first striking a hard bargain.

There was no large power near at hand, for the India of the Great Mogul was a decadent, dying empire, too weak even to make a gesture toward stamping out these scamps. The most they had to fear was an occasional Portuguese or Dutch man-of-war. France and Great Britain were too busy fighting one another in a different ocean to give much attention to the Red Sea Men.

Easily the most powerful organization in that part of the world was the East India Company, an English outfit, popularly called the John Company, which maintained its own private army and heavily cannoned navy. But even though the John Company did have extraordinary powers its charter provided that its armed forces could be used only for the protection of its own property, and therefore as long as the Red Sea Men left it alone—as they were mighty careful to do—the John Company could not exterminate them.

Thomas Tew was a Red Sea Man. He had tried to get a privateer's commission from his native state of Rhode Island in 1694, but had been turned down as a known ex-pirate; so he had gone on the account without further formality. The main virtue of a privateer's license to Tom Tew, as to so many others, was that such a paper made it easier to buy cannons. Tew was ferocious in a boarding party, and not given to displays of clemency, yet he was an idealist in his own way. He was forever concocting grandiose, utopian schemes for a more even distribution of the world's wealth. He was an early communist.

James Plantain was a Red Sea Man. He lived in grand style in a castle high in the hills, a castle guarded by splendidly liveried Negro slaves. His harem, made up of sloe-eyed beauties draped in stolen silks and aclank with stolen jewelry, was famous. But Plantain was homesick—though of course he could never go back—and he used to call those houris by homely names: Peg, Sue, Moll, Kate. It made him feel better.

John Avery, alias Henry Avery, alias Henry Bridgman, alias Long Ben, was a Red Sea Man, one of the noisiest, one of the smelliest.

He too had started as a privateer, first officer aboard of *Duke*, but in Cadiz Bay, disgusted by the inactivity of the skipper, he had talked the crew into a successful mutiny. Then he became captain and changed the name of the vessel, patriotically, to *Charles II*. The mutineers did not kill the real captain, but put him into a small boat, together with a handful of seamen who would have no truck with piracy, and shoved them toward shore.

Avery was a spectacular figure who loved flamboyant dress. He captured the public imagination, particularly in England, where tales were told about his princely establishment on St. Mary's. Then, too, odes and ballads were written about him; Daniel Defoe made him the principal character of his *The Piracies of Captain Singleton*, and Charles Johnson's play, *The Successful Pyrate*, admittedly based on the life and career of Avery, broke all records at the Drury Lane.

But Avery, like James Plantain, waxed homesick. He decided to try to cash in and sneak back. It would be a costly operation. He knew that. He went by way of Boston. It is not clear why; most pirates at that time would have gone by way of New York, where Governor Benjamin Fletcher was known to be not unfriendly. In Boston Avery was given short shrift. He was not arrested, but he was too "hot" to hold, and was hustled out, leaving behind him a sizable chunk of his fast-dwindling fortune.

He went to Ireland, to Dublin, where he sold a few more diamonds—he had reduced his swag almost wholly to diamonds—at a great loss. Then, very quietly, he crept back to Devon, his native shire, and took a small house in the country outside of Bristol, a place called Bideford. In London he was still at the height of his fame and talked about everywhere, but he lived very silently in Bideford, being understandably reluctant to disclose his identity while the world still thought him at sea. Avery was getting to be an old man now—he who had once taken the Great Mogul's own treasure ship, *Gunsway*, along with 100,000 pieces-of-eight and a large number of rich, ransomable pilgrims bound for Mecca. All he asked was to be allowed to die in peace.

But you can't eat diamonds. Desperate, after a while, he sent for certain merchants of Bristol, displayed the remaining stones, and told them who he was. How much would these diamonds fetch? The merchants hemmed and hawed. They took the gems and promised to look into the matter. He would hear from them, they said. He never did. Too late did John Avery learn that there are pirates on land as well as on sea. When he died there was barely enough money left to bury him.

William Mayes was one of the Red Sea Men. In 1694 Mayes, though he lived in New York, and though his past was by no means spotless, obtained a privateer's commission in Rhode Island, probably through political pull. His mother, Sarah, was a daughter of Sam Gorton, former

president (governor) of the colony. Mayes had *Pearl*, a
60-tonner, with 6 guns and 50 men. He made little pretense at real privateering, but went on the account almost
at once. It was getting to be a racket.

William Mayes was one of the men mentioned in the
commission awarded to William Kidd to stamp out pirates
along "the coasts of America," the others being Tom Tew,
John Ireland, and Thomas Wake.

Did Kidd, then, stamp out the pirates of St. Mary's? No.
He joined them.

Very early in the proceedings he was seen drinking with
one of the most notorious of the lot, John Culliford, and
when he did put out to sea again it was to stop all sorts of
private merchant vessels, searching them, often taking
goods from them. Also, he raided the Malabar Coast, saying that the vessels he robbed had French passes, which
made them fair game for a licensed American privateer.
But it was the custom at that time and in that part of the
world, as well as in the Atlantic, for vessels to carry two
sets of papers—one French, one British—as protection
against privateers. They would produce only the set that
would seem to apply. Kidd knew this perfectly well. He
also knew that the vessels he plundered were not, in fact,
French.

Off that same Malabar Coast he got a real bag, a large
ship called the *Quedagh Merchant,* bound from Bengal to
Surat (which she never reached) and loaded with silks,
muslins, sugar, iron, saltpeter, and gold. Kidd took the entire cargo. He also took the ship itself. This was how he
put down piracy.

The word got out, and orders were sent to Lord Bellomont, then in Boston, to arrest William Kidd if he dared to return, and to send him in chains to England. A royal proclamation of clemency to all pirates who would foreswear their past life and report themselves in named two notable exceptions—John Avery and William Kidd.

Kidd might have been disturbed by something that had happened fairly early in his cruise. He had exchanged harsh words with his chief gunner, William Moore, going so far as to call Moore "a lousy dog." To this Moore retorted "If I am a lousy dog, then it's you that made me so." This exchange seems harmless enough, if in questionable taste, but it threw Kidd into a rage. Red-faced, muttering to himself, he paced the deck a few times. He may have been drunk, for he was drinking a lot at that time. Anyway, he ended the quarrel by picking up an oaken, iron-bound bucket and hitting Moore on the head. He said later that he was only acting in self-defense. Anyway, Moore never did regain consciousness.

Perhaps rumors of his status reached Captain Kidd 'way out there in St. Mary's, or perhaps he was worried about the Moore affair and thought that a little immediate fixing would help. Or, perhaps again, he wished to get back to his wife and family. Anyway he did have a shipful of loot, the ship being the *Quedagh Merchant* which he had taken for his own, and with some (though by no means all) of his men he made for the West Indies. There he learned that the civilized world was indeed calling him a pirate. He still might have turned back to Madagascar, but he didn't. Doubtless he trusted his political influence. After all, his company boasted four Cabinet members.

He left the *Quedagh Merchant* somewhere—it was never clear where—and in a small sloop especially purchased for the purpose he made for Boston, on the way stopping at Gardiner's Island in Long Island Sound to leave off some more of the loot. This was recovered later, as was the loot still aboard the sloop, but the *Quedagh Merchant* loot never was located, at least officially.

Kidd had been gone for almost three years, during which time only occasional, stray, unsavory stories about him drifted back from the other side of the world. His return, understandably, caused a sensation. Stories about buried treasure—stories that have persisted ever since—started then and there.

He had written ahead to Lord Bellomont, promising to explain. It could be that he hoped to bribe his lordship, along with certain others. But the case was too open now. Besides the Cabinet was tottering, about to collapse, and simply couldn't risk another scandal. All of a sudden everybody was very righteous. Kidd and his associates were arrested and sent to England in chains.

He was tried early in 1701 at Old Bailey, and found guilty of piracy *and* of the murder of William Moore. He was hanged May 23 at Wapping Old Stairs, between high and low tides, another privateer gone wrong.

Ironically, William Kidd's rather shabby criminal exploits really did help to put down piracy. The scandal stimulated much new legislation. Privateering, too, was modified and more stringently regulated as a result.

5 ☆ CHAOS ON THE HIGH SEAS

Privateers were individualists. They liked to do things their own way, and resented regulation. Some in truth were downright misfits—and those were the ones who slipped over the line, becoming pirates.

Unlike navy vessels, privateers never had to fight anything close to their own size. They could run away if they thought running away the best course. They were not held down by onerous duties, like patroling or blockading an enemy port. They were entirely on their own, within the time and space limits imposed by their individual commissions, and they never kept a regular premapped course.

This encouraged boldness of imagination. Whatever else they might have been, the privateers were not in a rut. This also made for a great deal of confusion, a confusion that was not entirely the fault of the privateers themselves but was inevitable because of the nature of their job, and also because of their lack of cohesion. This confusion grew as privateering increased, from war to war. Some of the mistakes made at sea as a result of it were comic. Others were tragic.

In those days, of course, there were many more sea-crossing and coasting vessels than there are now, and though they were much smaller they were at the same time much more varied. Here are only a few of the types:

Bilander: a two-masted vessel, somewhat like a brig, but with the mainmast bent to the whole length of the yard, hanging at an angle of 45 degrees and the foremost lower corner made fast to a ring-bolt on deck.

Brigatine: a two-masted merchantman, square-rigged on the foremast and fore-and-aft rigged on the mainmast.

Frigate: a fast-sailing Navy craft, mounting 20 to 60 guns. Frigate-built vessels had the quarterdeck and fore-castle raised from the waist, in distinction to the galley-built boats which were flush the whole length. They were usually, though not invariably, rigged as ships.

Fly-Boat: a large, flat-bottomed, high-sterned Dutch vessel of 400-500 tons burden.

Gallot: a Dutch or Flemish trading vessel, with rounded ribs and almost flat-bottomed. She had no foremast but a mizzenmast right in the stern and used only to carry a sail to assist in the steering. The mainmast was sometimes square-rigged.

Galleass: the largest type of galley, castellated fore and aft and carrying three lateen-rigged masts and further propelled by 32 banks of oars, each bank containing two oars and each oar worked by six or seven slaves chained to it.

Galley: a vessel resembling a galleass but smaller, carrying two lateen-rigged masts and worked by 25 banks of oars. The term was also applied to any large, broad-built boat, flush from bow to stern.

Galleon: a large vessel with three or four decks, used almost exclusively by the Spaniards in their trade with the West Indies and their other American possessions. The galleon could be identified as Spanish—or almost certainly Spanish—from a good distance.

Hag-Boat: a frigate-built ship, with a narrow stern and deep waist. Hag-boats were largely used as colliers and for carrying heavy goods.

Ketch: a two-masted vessel of about 100 tons burden. She was square-rigged on the foremast and fore-and-aft rigged on the mainmast, which was considerably shorter than the foremast. Schooner-rigging for ketches was not introduced until about 1720.

Long-Boat: the largest boat accompanying a ship and usually furnished with mast and sails. Long-boats were sometimes decked and armed for short expeditions.

Pettiauger: also called "perriagua" or "piragua," this was a sort of large canoe composed of the trunks of two trees hollowed out and made into one boat. The term was also applied to a flat-bottomed boat or barge for shallow water, occasionally fitted with two masts.

Pink: a general name applied to any sailing ship with a very narrow stern.

Schooner: a two- or three-masted vessel fore-and-aft rigged on all masts.

Shallop: a term applied to almost any kind of open boat.

Sloop: a term used loosely, and there were various kinds of sloop afloat. The actual sloop was a one-masted vessel, fore-and-aft rigged with a gaff-mainsail and jib. The Navy, however, used the word differently. A Navy sloop might be ship-rigged, brig-rigged, even schooner-rigged; but it was never sloop-rigged.

Snow: the largest type of two-masted vessel. Mainmast and foremast were square-rigged; just abaft the mainmast was a small mast with its foot fixed in a block of wood on the quarter-deck and its head attached to the maintop. This mast carried a trysail.

Tall Ship: this phrase was employed to describe English-built craft which were usually short-hulled and tall-masted, in distinction to the large hulls and small spars of Spanish vessels.

Yawl: a small ship's boat, often fitted with a mast.

The galley and galleass were never seen on this side of the Atlantic. The frigate was distinctly a fighting vessel, but the term concerned the number of its guns and gun decks, not its hull or rig, which were conventional. There were also Navy sloops, which were quite different from merchant sloops and totally different from the modern sloop.

You will note that there is no "warship" in that list. The warship as such, the so-called "ship of the line," built only for the purpose of fighting, was just beginning to appear in the world. Even up to the time of the Revolution many of the vessels in the British and French navies, and all in our own, were converted merchantmen.

Nor was this conversion anything startling or radical in point of appearance. It consisted chiefly of strengthening the decks against recoil, piercing the bulwarks for guns, and installing the guns themselves. There were certain other interior changes, such as an enormously enlarged magazine and the building of powder hoists; but from the *outside*, at a short distance, except for the extra numbers of gun ports—virtually all vessels carried some guns, even in time of peace, and the ports of a war vessel could readily be masked—there was little to distinguish a warship from a merchantman. By the time you *could* make out the difference it might be too late.

The first thing you would see of an approaching vessel was her rig—her masts, sails, spars. There were many different kinds of rig, as we have already seen, but there was no kind that was distinctively military, just as there was no kind that was distinctly national—that is, in the Western world. Moreover, even if there had been such a distinction, the way vessels were passed back and forth, captured and recaptured again and again, sometimes five or six times in the course of a single war, would have obliterated the lines.

You ask, What about the flag? Couldn't you tell by that?

Now, it's an odd thing but vessels at sea in the old days did not fly national flags. These were kept for special events only—or for battle. When two strange ships met at sea and after examining one another decided at last to fight, the flags went up as the first broadside boomed, not before. It would have been considered the height of rashness for a master to show a stranger at sea who he was before they were within speaking-trumpet distance. It was even esteemed a perfectly good trick, an accepted *ruse de guerre*, to run up a false flag at the last moment, to pretend that you were something you weren't. This was done not only by privateers but by warships as well; so that customarily nobody believed anything—until the shooting had started and it was too late.

What's more, the sight of naval uniforms—and if you were close enough to make out an epaulette, even with a spy glass, you might be much too close—did not prove that the other vessel was a naval vessel. Privateers had been known to employ such window-dressing in the hope of overawing their opponent and causing him to strike his colors. *Rosebud* tried that very trick—without success—when she tangled with Robinson and Barney in *Pomona*.

Except for signs that two or three or more captains might agree upon for a single cruise—it was not unusual for them to hunt together—the privateers had no regular set of signals as navies did. They had no over-all understanding or organization, no admirals, no board of war, no central intelligence agency. They were separate kingdoms and seldom compared notes, for they did not even have one notable, favored eating place. They had no publication, no circulars, and no code of ethics. Not only did they have no standard wage-scale, they had no wages at all; both officers and crew depended upon prizes and if they caught nothing, they got nothing.

It was not at all unusual for one privateer to chase another all day—or even for two or three days if the nights were clear and she could be kept in sight—before they both discovered that they were of the same nationality or that they were on the same side in the war.

It was not even unknown for them to start to *fight*, though fortunately no such fight even went far. All the same, one well-delivered broadside from up close could sink a ship in a matter of minutes.

True, the privateer operated under a law, or was supposed to; but this law was changed from time to time and
from colony to colony, later from state to state. Bonds
were raised, requirements were stiffened. But the confusion at sea persisted and grew even worse.

Not only did the privateers fail to establish among themselves any set of signals, they did not even have any
agreement with their own navies.

Early in the War of 1812 the *U.S.S. Constitution* was
proceeding north toward Nova Scotia. This was just before
she met and sank the British frigate *Guerrière,* thus winning for herself immortal fame and the sobriquet of "Old
Ironsides." She sighted a small brig and made for it, not
wishing it to be known that she was in these waters. The
brig, understandably, ran.

Now, that brig was an American privateer fresh out of
Boston on the beginning of what he hoped would be a
short but prosperous cruise. He mounted fourteen guns,
brand-new ones, hard to come by in times like those, and
expensive. He knew of course that he was being chased
by a warship—there could be no doubt about *Constitution!*
—but he assumed that it was a British warship, a natural
assumption in the circumstances. The chase lasted all day,
and by the time the *Constitution* did manage to overhaul
the brig, the privateering skipper, frantically trying to
lighten his load and perhaps escape, had heaved twelve
of his fourteen guns overboard. After that, there was
nothing for him to do but go back to Boston for more.

6 ☆ IT COULD BE CALLED
A GOLD RUSH

Suppose that you are a man of means, looking for a place to invest your money, and your country has just gone to war? There was no stock exchange in America in these early days. Suppose you thought of privateering? What would you do? How would you go about it?

Well, first of all (if you did not happen to be a captain yourself) you must get a skipper. Discipline on American privateers was not as strict as it was aboard of naval vessels, but neither was it lax, and the captain was all-powerful, a man whose orders could not be appealed.

It would be well to look into this prospective captain's reputation among the foremast hands who had served under him as well as among the owners, his past employers. Many a sea skipper was all affability ashore but a very devil off soundings, a different man altogether.

A sullen crew might be all right aboard a merchantman, but a privateer needed alertness, smartness, a willingness to fight. The crew would be so large that the work would not be hard—which meant that even more depended upon the personality of the captain, since an idle sailor can be a dangerous sailor.

A privateer was always overcrowded when she set forth. There were several reasons for this.

Virtually all merchant vessels in war times were armed, and some skippers might elect to resist a privateer's attack. A deckful of men waving cutlasses and boarding pikes as the privateering vessel overtook its intended victim would go a long way toward discouraging such a decision. Just the sight of such a crowd might bring about a peaceful submission—saving time, trouble, and conceivably lives.

Though the privateer would sail with an empty hold it was hoped by everybody connected with her that this hold would soon be filled with a miscellaneous cargo taken from other vessels. Men were needed to move this cargo, and move it fast, before an enemy warship could heave into sight and spoil the whole operation.

Many prisoners might be taken, and men would be needed to guard them or to give them battle if they broke loose, as often happened.

Most important of all, whenever it was possible the seized vessel would be sent to an American port for condemnation. That meant a prize crew of anywhere from half a dozen to twenty-odd men, depending upon the size of the prize, would be needed to take her in. Thus a privateer might return from a successful cruise with only about one tenth the crew she had signed on.

Next, you would need the vessel. There would be a wide choice here in almost any port, though prices would go high as soon as the word got out—and it *would* get out—that you were preparing to outfit a privateer.

What *kind* of vessel should you buy? The type of rig this vessel carried doesn't really matter. It could be a sloop or a schooner, a brig or a barkentine. The big thing was speed. Above everything else, this vessel must be fast. Maneuverability might count too; and certainly this vessel should not have too deep a keel, for if you were chased you might want to take her up some shallow river or inlet where a warship couldn't follow. But speed is the first thing to look for, as it is the last.

Or perhaps you have a vessel of your own that can be converted? All sorts of men did own vessels or parts of vessels then.

Since you plan to crack on every inch of canvas she will hold, you must see to it that all her spars are sound, her mast or masts well and firmly stepped. This craft will be under a great strain.

There must be storage space for an exceptionally large supply of spare sails and running- and standing-gear. Chain shot, in a tussle, might carry away a crippling amount of your canvas and sheets and lines, and your very life could hang on the speed with which you made repairs.

Remember, too, that you will be carrying an extraordinarily large supply of shot and powder—much more than a mere merchant vessel. The powder in particular must be stowed low, yet not so low that it won't be easy to get at in a fight. Anti-fire construction will be one of your biggest costs.

If the privateer is to operate in tropical waters (this would be up to the captain, provided that the license was unlimited), she should have her bottom scraped, then sheathed with copper, which was not easy to get in

America. A fouled bottom would slow any vessel, no matter how much canvas she had cracked on.

In *appearance,* even after the conversion job has been done, your privateer at a slight distance will look like an ordinary, inoffensive merchantman. That's good. That's the way you want it to look.

The work of conversion should not take long, a couple of weeks at the most, for you'll drive the men night and day. You will have to pay through the nose, but you'll get a good job done.

Meanwhile, government vessels, Navy vessels, or, in colonial times, royal vessels, would be laid up for lack of repairmen, since the crown or the federal Congress could not possibly match the wages privateers paid in the shipyards.

In the War of 1812 all sorts of costly concessions and extra allowances had to be made to ship carpenters and builders to get them to go north to Lake Champlain and Lake Erie and build the fleets that scored such stunning victories under Macdonough and Perry. Even so, they were always short-handed at both places. Sailors could be *ordered* to the spot, but workmen had to be weedled.

Before you pierce too many gunports it might be well to make sure that you have or can immediately get the guns to go into them.

The number does not matter, nor is the size important, though they must not be too large for your vessel. A prolonged firing might tear her seams open. The British regulations as to the minimum number and size of the guns a privateer must carry were little respected on this side of the sea in colonial days, nor were state or congressional restrictions observed later. The American privateer pushed out as soon as he could and with whatever armament he had managed to get because he knew that the first thing he would take off a prize was her guns. In the Revolution a ketch called *Skunk*, commissioned by New Jersey, carried but two guns and twenty men, yet she took nineteen prizes—making the fortune of everybody aboard, not to mention the owners.

There were three types of naval guns. One, the columbiad, was not used on privateers, which mounted only long guns and carronades.

A long gun was heavy, and it used a heap of powder. It would carry far, and it was accurate. The carronade, on the other hand, was not accurate and it did not have a long range, but up close in a broadside it could throw a tremendous weight of iron; and the privateers, who liked to work close, preferred the carronade, but they took whatever they could get.

The carronade was not as heavy as the long gun, and not as big—it did not preempt as much room. It did not use nearly as much powder, though it could be reloaded at least as quickly. And if it had to be jettisoned, like the guns of that brig the *Constitution* chased, then not as much was lost, for you could buy five or six carronades—when you *could* buy them—for the price of one good long gun.

You need not be afraid of revealing your mission. There was no disgrace connected with the financing of privateers. In Rhode Island, and particularly at Newport, it was a way of life. Governor Benedict Arnold has been mentioned. Thomas Paine, one of the biggest investors there, was a founder of Trinity Church, which still stands. In neighboring Massachusetts the house of Cabot, then as now to be mentioned only with bated breath, had extensive privateering interests. So did the house of Crowninshield.

You apply either for a letter of marque or a privateer's license, at a vice-admiralty court. In colonial times each provincial governor had vice-admiralty powers, and he could and did issue letters of marque and privateering commissions in time of war, either directly or through somebody to whom he delegated that power. In the Revolution the governors retained this authority, and the Continental Congress issued such papers as well.

The Constitution of the United States authorizes Congress "to declare War, grant letters of Marque and Reprisal, and make Rules concerning Captures on Land and Water" (Article 1, Section 8), by implication taking this power from the individual states. After its formal ratification in 1788, this work was done by agents of the federal government, who, however, were to be found in every port.

A letter of marque was carried by a merchantman who did not plan to rove, but who wanted to be able to protect himself if attacked. A privateering commission, on the other hand, was issued to a captain who had no thought of carrying cargo—at first.

Let us say that you seek a privateering commission. If your background is not murky, you should have little trouble getting it, though of course you will be obliged to post a bond to the value of your vessel as an insurance against possible future claims, and there will be sundry lawyers' and clerks' and officials' fees. These men too want to cash in on the madness of privateering, just like the ordnance merchants and the shipbuilders, and they can always threaten you with delay, with red tape. Delay is what you most dread, and you'll pay anything to avert it, for privateering is a fever that burns in the blood. Like all the others you believe that if you can only get out there early enough you will make millions.

It's like a gold rush. Indeed in a manner of speaking it *is* a gold rush.

Your license may limit your roving, or it may be unlimited. However it is almost sure to have a *time* limit on it, and in any event it would automatically expire when peace was declared. If you should happen to be at sea when this happens, it might be a month or more, even three or four months, before you hear of it—though as a rule privateering voyages were not long. In that case, and if you took a prize or prizes after the time peace was declared but before you yourself had heard of it, that prize or those prizes will not be libelled and must be returned in good condition.

Meanwhile your captain is raising a crew. He will, of course, pick his own mate or mates, and a sailing master as well if he carries one, though most captains are their own sailing masters. As for the seamen, he will not have to go into the country and beat a drum for recruits, or offer free drinks to enlistees. The press gang, that ugly medieval hangover, never was resorted to on this side of the sea. No, the sailors will come to the skipper, once the word is out. They'll come hat in hand, pleading. All the captain has to do is pick the best men and be careful that he does not get any deserters from the Navy, because the service brass already hate him enough as it is.

"There is at this time 5 Privateers fitting out here, which I suppose will take 400 men," William Whipple of the officer procurement committee wrote to Josiah Bartlett from Portsmouth, New Hampshire, at the time when John Paul Jones was there desperately trying to raise enough men to permit him to take out his soon-to-become-famous *Ranger*. "Besides all this, you may depend no public ship will ever be manned while there is a privateer fitting out. The reason is plain: Those people who have the most influence with Seamen think it their interest to discourage the Public service, because by that they promote their own interest, viz., Privateering."

This was true not only at Portsmouth (which, by the way, was then called Falmouth) but everywhere else in America. The Navy, too, granted prize money, breaking each prize into twenty equal pieces, of which three went to the captain; two to the sea lieutenants and sailing master; two to the marine officers, surgeon, gunner, purser, bosun, carpenter, master's mates, and chaplain; three to the midshipmen, surgeon's mates, captain's clerk, schoolmaster, steward, sailmaker, bosun's mates, master-at-arms, armorer, and coxswain; three to the gunner's yeomen, bosun's yeomen, quartermasters, quarter gunners, coopers, sailmaker's mates, sergeants and corporals of the marines, drummer, fifer, and extra petty officers; and seven parts to the seamen, ordinary seamen, marines, and boys. Moreover, this would be paid even if you sank the prize or burned her.

This Navy regulation concerning prize money was a

model one for most of the American privateers, who, however, drew up a separate contract for each cruise.

All the same, you had a much better chance of hitting it big if you sailed with a privateer. Or at least, that's what men thought. Everybody loves to gamble.

Now you must make up articles of agreement, and this can be quite a process.

As far as you can, you cover everything. The vessel and all its present and future contents, including all prizes, are divided into "lays," just as was done on so many fishing vessels and later was to be done on sealers and whaling ships. These lays usually are sixty-four in number, of which "the ship and her owners," almost always including the skipper, get half. The other half goes to the officers and men according to a complicated sliding scale of values. There are usually clauses providing extra payments to men who lose an arm, a leg, and so on, or who are killed. Often there is also a proviso that "if any man coward" in action he shall lose his lay.

The men all sign this at last, or make their marks.

You will be obliged, of course, to carry a very heavy supply of provisions and water, since you have so big a crew and hope to have so many prisoners.

But your voyage, however attended by good fortune, will not be a long one. Privateering always was a hit-and-run business.

So now you are ready to sail—and God help you!

7 ☆ THE MOSQUITO FLEET

The colonial wars—King William's, Queen Anne's, the others—made up a carnival for the American privateer.

These wars were fought for remote political reasons of which he knew little and cared less. *And* they were fought far away. The skipper of an American privateering vessel, the mates and hands as well, did not have to worry about their wives and children who were perfectly safe at home. No enemy would descend upon such comparatively barren shores when there were prizes like the West Indian islands so near at hand—and so weak. Except for a few daring, eccentric pioneers who had pushed inland—(nine-tenths of the seamen in the American privateers lived on or within a few miles of the coast), the colonists no longer feared redskin raids. No taxes or irksome restrictions were imposed upon them as a direct result of these wars, which, as far as they were concerned, were a series of romps. They brought no responsibilities; but the training was fine, and the pickings were good.

The French and Indian War (the Seven Years War) had to be taken more seriously. There were special taxes—

taxes imposed by the colonial legislatures, to be sure, but they had to be paid anyway. For the first time a large force of British regulars, under General Braddock, was landed in America, and spirited efforts were made to swell their ranks with colonists. The press gang was not resorted to, but sometimes it was hard to stay away from those recruiting sergeants. The redskin was as far off as ever, but he was acting ugly, and for the first time in many years, egged on by his French allies, he was showing signs of coming back.

Americans, somewhat scared, played an active part in the French and Indian War, both on the field and at sea.

Yet truly it was not until the outbreak of the Revolution that Americans had to concern themselves with matters maritime, with the task of organizing their own Navy. And the inspiration for this, as much as it could be said to be from one man, came from, unexpectedly, George Washington.

He had no seafaring background. True, his estate, Mount Vernon, had been named after an admiral, but George Washington himself had not named it. He had no association with ships. He lived inland. He had never been to Europe, and his only experience in voyaging was a trip to the West Indies with his sick half-brother Lawrence (who died soon afterward), when George himself was still in his teens. That voyage could hardly have been a happy one, since besides the fact that he was probably seasick much of the time (he had a queasy stomach in the best of circumstances), he contracted smallpox down there and all but died of it, his face being marked for life.

Yet this same man displayed an uncommon interest in

sea warfare and did everything that he could to get an American Navy started.

A real Navy, a regular, uniformed, disciplined force, was what Washington wanted. But privateering was helped indirectly by this interest of his and, for a little while, it looked as though the privateers, the irregulars, would run the entire show.

When the day of Lexington and Concord ended, the British redcoats, dazed, dusty, and dead tired, stumbled back to Charleston; then they went on to Boston, which was immediately surrounded by the angry buzzing American militiamen, who started a siege.

It was an odd sort of siege, not carried on along conventional lines, as it would have been in Europe, with parallels and redoubts and redans and covered ways and half-moons and counterscarps and terrepleins and all the rest of it, but consisting only of a cluster of disconnected red-necked rawboned farmers who squatted everywhere and dared the British to come out. This the British very sensibly declined to do.

They were not completely surrounded however. The side of the sea was open. To bring in all their supplies by ship, in the summertime when the land was filled with orchards and vegetable gardens and cattle and swine, was costly, but they could afford it. And Concord and Lexington had taught them that to go out and raid those stables and orchards might prove a great deal more costly in the long run. Meanwhile, they had sent for reinforcements.

Washington strove to regularize the siege, and he sent Henry Knox to Ticonderoga in northern New York to bring down a whole train of cannons captured there by

Ethan Allen and Benedict Arnold, "in the name of the great Jehovah and the Continental Congress." Then Washington turned his attention to the sea.

It was shameful, he agreed, that the British should be allowed to come and go as they pleased on the bay side of Boston. But he had no navy; nor is a national navy the sort of thing that you can organize and equip in a few weeks or even months. Washington did the next best thing, the best *immediate* thing. Paying them from his own military chest, he authorized certain army or militia officers with nautical backgrounds to pick up coasting vessels here and there, hastily arm them, and then go out near the entrance of Boston harbor and see what happened.

A great deal did happen.

These men could not be called privateers, because they fought at the public expense, but they worked with such privateers as there were, and they must certainly, by any definition, be called *irregulars*. They were "sea partisans," for a little while. They were sometimes called a marine militia, sometimes a voluntary navy; and they did telling work there in the first few months of the struggle, catching the British off balance.

For instance, on November 29, 1775, *Lee*, a vessel commissioned by Washington himself, though owned by the colony of Massachusetts, brought into Cape Ann roads the British *Nancy* with 2000 muskets and 2000 bayonets, 3000 rounds of shot for 12-pounders, some gunpowder, and 50 carcasses, or fire shells. Here was a welcome cargo indeed! Until this time there had been hardly a bayonet in the whole Continental Army.

That same small vessel soon afterward, in the company of *Defense,* Captain Seth Harding, master, and three small privateers with which they had joined company, chased two transports into the harbor at Nantasket, and took them there, together with their cargo of 200 regular British redcoats, intended as reinforcements to the Boston garrison.

The next day the same vessels went outside again and captured yet another British transport with yet another 100 redcoats. And soon afterward the armed sloop *Warren* duplicated this feat.

It was no thunderous victory, but at least the British had been served notice. This would not be as easy a squashing party as it had seemed at first. Hereafter they had better detail a warship when they wished to send soldiers across the sea.

The British Navy after the French and Indian War had been whittled down dismally, and weakened. But even at its lowest, it was quite capable of whipping, with one hand tied behind its back, the absurd conglomeration of cockleshells that the revolting colonists could send against it.

Cockleshells? No, say rather mosquitoes. They performed that function; they were pesky and persistent. And within their limits, those first American sea partisans got good results. At least they held the line for a little while.

8 ☆ FRANCE GETS INTO
THE FIGHT

This mosquito period, the period of offshore privateering, soon passed. Then the amateurs became full-time professionals, and their patriotic zeal was to some extent replaced by a determination to make money at all costs. It is only fair to add, however, that the American privateers in the Revolution were an exceptionally patriotic group, as privateers went. They often took nonpaying risks to get information, prisoners, or goods for the government.

There were several reasons for this change.

First of all, Britain, worried—for trade was the very lifeblood of the nation—began to arm its merchantmen or to cause them to sail only in convoy, protected by warships. Obviously then open boats, men with pikes, no longer were enough to take such prizes.

Initially, commissions for privateering were issued only by the individual colonies, and were of doubtful validity, but after a few months of hesitation the Continental Congress itself, on March 23, 1776, resolved "that the inhabitants of these colonies be permitted to fit out armed vessels to cruise on the enemies of these United Colonies," and followed up this resolution, April 3, by authorizing the issuance of actual commissions. These were at once popular, for they were taken rather more seriously than the colonial commissions. Privateers could hardly be called timid men, but it was only human to wish to avoid any suggestion of piracy, since pirates were hanged. As it turned out the British never did hang any captured American privateer, though they often threatened to, and they certainly did not coddle such prisoners.

The law authorizing these commissions was strict for a privateering law of the time, and contained many provisions about reporting prizes, taking care of prisoners, and other matters. One curious clause stated that at least one-third of a privateering crew must be "landsmen." Perhaps this was meant to protect the new Navy from having *every one* of its men drained off. The bond provision was somewhat higher than that set by most of the colonies—$5000 for a vessel under 100 tons, $10,000 for a vessel of 100 tons or more—but this did not deter any of the gamblers. That very same year of 1776 Rhode Island alone, the smallest of the colonies, sent out a total of fifty-seven privateers; and that was only the beginning of the flood.

However, the greatest reason for the swift spread of privateering was the attitude of the French.

After a humiliating defeat at the hands of Great Britain in the French and Indian War, France was eager for revenge. From the beginning she had been strongly in favor of the American colonists' cause, scarcely troubling to conceal this from the world. Soon, it was certain, she would get into this fight herself; meanwhile, she was doing everything she could to help, short of war. Through the agency of a "Spanish" firm named Rodrique Hortalez et Cie., located in the huge former Dutch Embassy in Paris, and operated by that ebullient watchmaker, financier, musician, and author of "The Barber of Seville," Pierre Augustin Caron de Beaumarchais, she was sending the colonies all sorts of arms and gunpowder, though repeating officially that she was doing no such thing. And not merely Lafayette but dozens, scores, even hundreds of other young Frenchmen, titled and otherwise, were pouring across the Atlantic to take up arms with the Continentals. When Britain protested, the French Foreign Minister Vergennes dryly pointed out that the French "had a turn for adventure."

France soon went even further. She let it be known, unofficially, that her ports would be open to American privateers.

The Treaty of Utrecht, signed in 1713 by Britain and France at the end of the War of the Spanish Succession (Queen Anne's War), still was binding upon both nations. It forbade either to permit the enemies of the other to use her ports for privateering. So now Britain protested quite properly. Vergennes replied that the French, being humane, could not bring themselves to bar from their harbors any vessel in distress. Thereafter every American privateer who needed to sell his prizes or to restock his larder or his powder magazine, blandly announced that he was "in distress."

The French themselves had a long tradition of privateering on a grand scale. The celebrated Jean Bart of Dunkirk on one morning—the morning of Monday, September

25, 1690—had taken four separate Hanseatic ships and had held them for an on-the-spot cash ransom of 39,000 livres. Ducasse and DePointis got 20,000,000 livres ransom out of Cartagena a few years later. Dugnay-Tronin, who in 1711 took Rio de Janiero after defeating the whole Portuguese fleet, was ennobled for having captured sixteen men-of-war and no fewer than three hundred merchantmen. Oh, the privateer was a hero in France! But as long as they stayed out of the War of the American Revolution the French had to restrain themselves.

Yet France was benefited, perhaps even more than America, by this policy of assisting "distressed" vessels. The American privateers, who otherwise would have had great difficulty operating so far from home, found that with the aid of French supplies and a French market they could make things so hot for Great Britain in the English Channel that insurance rates soared and the merchants of London took to shipping their goods in French bottoms, which, being technically neutral, would not be touched. This was truly a sardonic situation; it made Frenchmen chuckle while the British lion lashed its tail in rage.

The laws set down by Congress for American privateers said that all prisoners must be treated well, on pain of loss of license. These prisoners, on reaching port, became the property of the federal government, which was saving them for exchange purposes. There were a great many such prisoners. When the enemy moved a whole regiment across the sea it was, of course, protected by one or more warships, but again and again small single dispatch boats were captured with a handful of colonels and majors or a holdful of sergeants and privates, replacements. These usually came in small batches, but the total number was tremendous. The Army's acquisitions of prisoners were spectacular—at Trenton, Saratoga, Yorktown—yet the Navy and the privateers, and especially the privateers, took more than these. As a result in 1779 Great Britain at last felt herself obliged to sign a cartel for the exchange of these and other prisoners, something that until then she had stoutly refused to do, since it smacked of recognizing the damn rebels as an independent country.

Then at last, when she was good and ready, France did declare war on Great Britain, and on July 17, 1778, signed a Treaty of Amity and Commerce with "the United States of North America," the first nation formally to recognize this country. That treaty is long. It consists of many clauses, of which only Article XVII need detain us here, for it provided in the fullest terms that each nation should be free to use the ports of the other for privateering purposes. That did not seem significant at the time, for it had been taken for granted. It was to become very significant indeed a few years later, as we shall see.

9 ☆ YOU CAN GO HOME NOW

To a regular Navy man, battle was opportunity. It might mean a citation, a medal. It might mean promotion or prize money. Assuredly, and whatever the outcome, it would mean valuable experience; it would help him in his profession. The Navy officer never turned away from battle, but sought it out, eagerly.

With the privateers it was different. To a privateer, fighting was no more than an occasional unfortunate necessity. He tried to keep it at a minimum. A show of force, not a struggle, was usually all that he needed. He wasn't seeking glory for his country or for himself; he was seeking profits for his owners, and common sense told him to keep from being hurt or his vessel damaged, whenever this was possible. He *would* fight, oh, yes! But fighting was a sideline, not the central part of his business.

There were exceptions. Every now and then some privateer would be cornered and have to slug his way out, and every now and then, too, one of them would challenge a bigger and more heavily armed vessel, even in some cases a war vessel, for all the world as though he just needed the exercise.

In Salem, Massachusetts, during the Revolution, as later during the War of 1812, privateering was a way of life, an accepted and highly acceptable condition. It occupied almost everybody's time and attention.

Jonathan Haraden lived in Salem, when he wasn't at sea, though he had been born in nearby Gloucester. A quiet, efficient man, cool in action, never flustered, he had far more than his share of fighting.

He was one of the first of the "nautical militiamen," a lieutenant aboard *Tyrannicide*, a small but exceedingly active vessel. After taking sundry prizes near home, and finding among them some dispatches valuable to General Washington, *Tyrannicide*, on March 29, 1779, came upon the British brig of war *Revenge*, off Bermuda, and instantly attacked. They were well matched, and, locked with grappling hooks, they had been at it for two hours hammer-and-tongs, when the Britisher at last struck.

It was Jonathan Haraden, a skipper now, commanding the 180-ton *General Pickering*, again out of Salem, who fought one of the most sensational sea duels in the history of privateering. *General Pickering* had aboard a cargo of sugar for Bilboa, a Spanish port on the Bay of Biscay. In the early days of the war the Spaniards at Bilboa had been leery of American privateers, and had even come near to hanging one of them as a pirate. Lately, however, they had been more accommodating; they did not draw any national line, but welcomed English *and* American *and* French alike. After selling her sugar *General Pickering* wanted to see what she could pick up in the Channel.

She was set upon in mid-ocean by a British cutter which greatly outweighed her, and there was a running fight of several hours, *General Pickering* in the end being saved only by the coming of night.

Another night, soon afterward, was helpful to *General Pickering*, when under cover of darkness and not far from the Bay of Biscay she all but collided with the British armed brig *Golden Eagle*. Thinking fast, Captain Haraden called upon the brig to strike instantly or he would sink her, for he identified his own vessel as "a United States frigate of the heaviest class." At any time this might have been a disconcerting message, but now when John Paul Jones was sinking warships large and small all around the island of Great Britain it was downright alarming to a skipper who could not get a good look at his neighbor.

A frigate at that range, even a comparatively light one, *could* have knocked him out of the water with a single broadside, in a matter of seconds. So without firing a shot, the Englishman surrendered. He expressed his humiliation later, when he went aboard *General Pickering* as a prisoner and saw how small she really was, about the size of his own brig. Still the trick was a fair one, as seamen looked at things in those days. Haraden put a prize crew aboard of *Golden Eagle* and ordered her to follow him into Bilboa.

As they approached that port a large vessel, bristling with gun ports, was seen striving to get out, for the wind was very light. Haraden asked the captain of *Golden Eagle* if he knew her. The captain did. She was a privateer out of London, *Achilles*, much larger than *General Pickering* and with forty-two guns and 140 men. (*General Pickering* had 16 guns, 6-pounders, and 45 men.) Now, the English captain might have been saying this only in order to scare Haraden. So the privateer only replied, "Well, I won't run away from her," and kept his course.

They could not come together that night nor all the next day, because of tricky winds. It was a time of great strain, a situation calculated to rasp the nerves of even the most stolid. It was made endurable in the American vessel by the demeanor of Captain Haraden, who might have been in his own parlor back in Salem, waiting to be called to supper. Haraden saw that everything that needed doing was done, but he never raised his voice, never fussed. He ate well, and slept well; and his men, seeing this, remained steady.

It was clear to those on land that these two vessels were

preparing to fight, and the word spread. Spaniards came hurrying into Bilboa from all over the countryside. The shore and the streets were black with them. They leaned out of windows, breathless. They sat on rooftops. They climbed into trees. Hundreds of them even pushed out in small boats to get a better look.

There was distinctly a holiday atmosphere about Bilboa and its offing that early morning of June 4, 1780, when *Achilles* and *General Pickering* at last sailed within range of one another. And the spectators were given a good show.

It lasted for more than three hours. *Achilles* wished to close, to grapple, but Haraden kept away from her. *Achilles*, being so much larger, made a better target, and again and again, even in that light air, sometimes using sweeps, or long oars, Haraden managed to get under her stern and rake her. He didn't miss a trick. The English had plenty of spirit, but the American gunnery was better; and at last *Achilles* had to quit. She didn't strike, but, badly crippled, she backed away.

All the while Jonathan Haraden had been as calm as though, as one of his men put it, "he was only in a snow storm."

The crowd went wild with delight, waving and shouting for a long while, milling about the victor in their boats; and when a little later the still unsmiling Haraden went ashore to see about the sale of that sugar, he was treated to the sort of ovation that ordinarily would have been given only to a successful bull fighter.

Incidentally, Haraden encountered three armed merchantmen on his way home. They were sailing together for purposes of protection, and since each was about his own size they could have slashed him to ribbons if they had *stayed* together. But in an exhibition of consummate seamanship, Haraden cut them apart and took them one by one. It was a great day in Salem when he got back.

Sometimes called the "Salamander" because of his ability to stand fire, Jonathan Haraden was to have yet more spirited sea duels before the end of the year, and he never lost a ship. But that bright windless morning outside of Bilboa, while thousands watched, would always remain the high point of his life.

10 ☆ FIGHT TO THE END

The surrender of Cornwallis at Yorktown on October 19, 1781, did not end the Revolutionary War. The British still had two armies in America. They still had large naval forces in American waters, forces capable of imposing an effective blockade on large portions of the coast. And they still occupied New York, Wilmington, Charleston, and Savannah.

It was not until almost a year later, in Paris, that peace was agreed upon, and it was not until April 19, 1783, that this agreement was ratified and proclaimed.

As far as the land forces were concerned, Yorktown did indeed mark the end of the war; but the situation at sea was different. The infant United States Navy had been mostly taken or sunk, and what few warships remained in commission were bottled in ports they did not dare to leave. The privateers, however, had never been so active. Perhaps sensing that there would not be much more time, they swarmed everywhere.

De Grasse, after having helped so much, had withdrawn to the West Indies, where he was having trouble of his own.

The valuable (if ugly) Dutch port of St. Eustatius ("Statia"), one of the Leeward Islands, very popular as a refitting stop for privateers and smugglers and a reshipping center for at least half of the French muskets and ammunition en route to the American colonies, had fallen to the British Navy, which dismantled it. And now at the tail end of the war the convoy system was becoming increasingly effective, and such British merchantmen as did sail alone were much more heavily armed.

Nevertheless, the American privateers, as though in a frenzy, redoubled their activities.

Though generally larger in size and more heavily armed than privateering vessels had been at the beginning of the war, they now ranged all the way from the 2-gun, 15-man *Chance*, out of Philadelphia (which on June 12, 1780, off Sandy Hook fought and captured the British sloop *Comet*, 10 guns, 50 men), to the 24-gun *Congress* with a crew of 200 under Captain George Geddes of Philadelphia (which on September 6, 1781, off the coast of Georgia encountered the 16-gun British sloop *Savage*).

The *Savage* was herself a privateer, and the skipper, a man named Sterling, used somewhat unconventional methods. He had a vessel of slight draft and liked to poke into small bays and up rivers in the southern part of the Atlantic Coast. He would spot a plantation house and turn away, but after dark he would land a raiding party that would plunder that house. This was a lucrative business but it did not make him well liked. So when the dawn of that memorable September day off Georgia showed him that he was sharing the sea with a larger American vessel, Captain Sterling quite properly decided to run away.

But *Congress* not only was heavier, she was also faster. By half past ten she had drawn close enough to the English privateer to open up with her bow chasers, long-range guns. By eleven she was near enough to open fire with her carronades as well, and soon afterward even with muskets and pistols.

There was nothing left for Sterling to do but stand and battle it out. And this he did—extremely well.

The fight was so fierce and so close that men on both sides were scorched by the flashes from opposing cannons. A few, in their rage, even picked up small balls and *threw* them at the enemy.

When it became clear that under that terrible pounding *Congress* was becoming unmanageable, Captain Geddes had her fall back out of range for repairs.

There was no worry that the Britisher might run away. *Savage* was already a wreck, her skipper dead, both mates wounded, her mast down, her deck a shambles, her rudder shot away, her sails in ribbons.

Nevertheless, when a hastily patched *Congress* returned to the fray, *Savage* opened up on her.

Toe-to-toe again, gunnel-to-gunnel, they slugged it out

for half an hour. Then it became plain to Captain Geddes that only a boarding party could convince those stubborn Englishmen they were licked.

He gave the order. The men assembled in the waist, where pikes and cutlasses were passed out. Sleeves were rolled up, belts tightened, bare feet dipped into sand.

But at this moment the bosun, as the senior surviving officer—*Savage*'s flag had long since been shot down, so he couldn't strike his colors—waved his cap in a signal of surrender. The guns fell silent.

The British casualties were thirty-two, the American thirty.

That victory, however, did the *Congress* no good, for immediately after the fight a British frigate came along and scooped up both the wounded ships and sent them to Charleston. *Congress* was taken into the British Navy as the *Duchess of Cumberland*. She was filled with prisoners of war and dispatched to England. She never got there. She was wrecked off Newfoundland.

Some of the hottest fights were between privateers, as when, in February of 1781, the 16-gun brig *Holker* from Philadelphia took on the British cutter *Hypocrite,* similarly weaponed, and after a furious fifteen-minute fight caused her to strike.

Or the *Viper* of Boston, skippered by Captain William Williams, on October 22, 1780, off Cape Hatteras battled and beat the *Hetty* out of New York, each, again, with 16 guns.

An even bloodier affair occurred on the high seas in January of 1781 when the 18-gun ship *Pilgrim* from out of

Boston (there were also in this war *Pilgrim* privateers from Connecticut, Pennsylvania, and Virginia) met and tackled the 22-gun British *Mary,* which was more heavily manned. *Pilgrim's* men were veteran fighters, for their vessel had a long record of prizes. In time they prevailed, but both vessels, at the end, were virtually wrecks.

Not all privateering skippers were as lucky as Jonathan Haraden. To young Captain John Manly, high on the list of U.S. Navy officers early in the war, a stunning career seemed certain. Alas, there was no vessel for him to command, the greater part of the Navy being at that time under construction. So rather than wait around doing nothing he accepted command of a privateer, *Cumberland,* with 16 guns. Before he could accomplish anything with this vessel it was taken by a British frigate of overwhelming strength, and Manly and his men were thrown into jail in the Barbadoes. They escaped, and made their way back to Boston, where Manly was given another privateer to command, the 20-gun *Jason.* Twice he had narrow escapes in this ill-fated vessel, once being saved from a British fleet by fog, the other time by a violent gale that dismasted him off the Isle of Shoals, New Hampshire. While supervising the rigging of jury masts he was threatened by a mutiny (he seems not to have been a popular skipper) which he put down almost singlehandedly. Nothing daunted, he set out for the English Channel, where the pickings were supposed to be best. Off Newfoundland, at night, he came upon the British frigate *Surprise.* Greatly outweighed, he should have run; but he made about. He fought for hours, until his men refused any longer to handle their guns, refused even to come up on deck. And only then did he surrender.

So once again John Manly went to prison—this time in England. Just before the end of the war he was exchanged, and hastened back to Boston to receive his finest command yet—a regular Navy frigate, the 32-gun *Deane*.

In this he hurried south, praying that there would still be time to take some prizes—only to run spang into a whole British war fleet. Close-pressed, he took refuge in the French harbor of Port Royal, Martinique (now Fort-de-France). The British stationed a blockading squadron outside, beyond the range of the fort's guns, so that John Manly could not move; and that is where *he* finished the war.

The pride of the American privateering force was a late-comer, *General Washington*, which carried 20 six-pounders. She took to the sea from Boston early in 1780, and soon encountered a British ship of 18 guns in company with a 6-gun brig. The ensuing battle lasted for two hours, and it was fierce. *General Washington* suffered three killed and three wounded. Four of her guns were dismounted, and her mainmast was shot away, so that she could not maneuver well. The British vessels at last decided that they'd had enough, and withdrew, while *General Washington* limped home for repairs.

On her second time out *General Washington* at dawn one day found herself in the very middle of a British fleet under Admiral Arbuthnot. It was the sort of thing that happened all the time, and there was nothing to do but surrender.

The British liked *General Washington*, for she was

fast, and they took her into their own Navy, changing her name to *General Monk*. Under the redoubtable Captain Rodgers, R.N., she was a notable commerce killer, ranging the coast from Maine to Florida and taking, in a year and a half, more than sixty prizes.

Then on April 8 of 1782 she was standing off and on between Cape Henlopen, Delaware, and Cape May, New Jersey—in other words, at the entrance to Delaware Bay—in the company of a few small Tory privateers from New York. They were waiting for a convoy of merchant vessels due to come down the Delaware River, hoping to get some of them as prizes before they could break up and scatter across the face of the sea. *General Monk* would not trouble herself with chasing these merchantmen—she'd leave that to the privateers. She was intent upon a rumor that the merchants of Philadelphia had fitted out an escorting vessel.

The merchants of Philadelphia had done just that. The *Hyder Ally* was pierced for sixteen 6-pounders and carried a crew of 120, some of these being backswoodsmen from Buck's County, Pennsylvania, brought along for their crack shooting. The skipper of *Hyder Ally* was Lieutenant Joshua Barney, U.S.N., who like so many other Navy officers could not get a command in the service and wished to keep busy. The Philadelphia merchants could not have picked a better man.

For Barney instantly grasped the situation and never hesitated. He ignored the privateers, and, though his vessel was much smaller, made immediately for Rodgers and the *General Monk*.

Rodgers, for his part nothing loth, went right for the *Hyder Ally*.

For a little while it looked as though each was planning to lay himself alongside of the other, for boarding and hand-to-hand fighting. Captain Rodgers asked nothing better than this, since his men outnumbered Barney's. Aboard of *General Monk* the quartermaster's mates began to pass out pikes and cutlasses.

But Barney swerved suddenly to starboard, and since his vessel was slightly ahead of the other this brought about a collision—which was exactly what Barney wanted.

General Monk's bowsprit and jib gear got entangled with the *Hyder Ally*'s foremast rigging. There she was: she couldn't go ahead, she couldn't back away. If Rodgers still meant to board he would have to do it over the length of his own bowsprit, always a perilous proceeding, and Barney had provided against this with boarding nets.

More important, Barney now could hammer *General Monk* with every one of his starboard guns, and at point-blank range. In naval parlance, he "raked" the Britisher— that is, he shot his cannonballs the whole length of the enemy vessel, where they would do the most harm, kill the most men. Rodgers, on the other hand, head-on, could not bring a single one of his broadside guns to bear, only a few small swivels and bow chasers.

In addition, there were those Bucks County marksmen, with a whole deck to sweep. Loading and firing, they picked off their targets as coolly as squirrel hunters.

The battle lasted half an hour, and when *General Monk* struck her casualties were counted at twenty killed and thirty-three wounded. *Hyder Ally* had four killed, eleven wounded.

Joshua Barney did not even pause to ask the name of his enemy but threw a prize crew aboard, chopped off the *General Monk*'s bowsprit, and went right after the fleeing privateers, none of which he caught. Congress gave him an engraved sword for this exploit.

That fight between Cape May and Cape Henlopen was by almost any definition the last battle of the American Revolution. There were to be skirmishes later, but this was the last real battle.

The privateers, however, went right on raiding, hunting. Altogether in that war they captured or destroyed at least three times as many enemy ships as did the Navy. Their bag included sixteen vessels of war, an opponent your privateer ordinarily shunned.

Though there are no official figures, it has been estimated that the American privateers kept between 200 and 450 vessels in active duty all through the Revolution, and many more at the end than in the middle. At the end of the war too there were about 9000 American colonists at sea or about to go to sea as privateers. George Washington himself did not always have that many soldiers under his command.

But when at last peace was ratified and proclaimed, the American privateers, to a man, sailed home. There was no question, this time, of "peace making pirates." They'd had enough.

11 ☆ THE BOY WONDER

France was changing, violently. The throne teetered, it wobbled, and at last it fell. Louis XVI was beheaded. France had become a republic; and she announced that she was about to replace her ambassador to the United States, Jean Baptist de Ternant, with Edmond Charles Genêt.

Here was an extraordinary person, Genêt. He was not, as had been said of his serious-minded young countryman the Marquis de Lafayette, "a statue walking around looking for a pedestal to stand on." No, Genêt always had been on a pedestal, at least in his own eyes.

A child prodigy, who at the age of five could spout Greek and English, he was soon to learn five other languages, in every one of which he was, to put it mildly, fluent. At fifteen he published his own translation from the Swedish of a biography of Eric XIV. He was also a scientist and an inventor.

He was an ardent Republican, and when he was sent to Russia he at first delighted Catherine the Great, for he was tall and handsome. But when he began to spout revo-

lutionary talk the lady turned cold, and soon he was asked
to leave. Back in Paris the Girondins hailed him a hero:
to be snubbed by an empress was, to those people, an
honor.

When he sailed for America Genêt had with him something that could cause untold trouble—a bagful of privateering commissions.

France had just launched the second of her wars of the
Revolution. The first had been against Austria and Prussia,
neither of which was much of a commercial nation, in the
seagoing sense, and so this contest had not involved the
new United States. The second war was different. It was
against Great Britain, Holland, and Spain, all maritime
nations.

The French Revolution had been watched carefully
from this side of the sea, and on the whole with approval,
even enthusiasm. President Washington's Secretary of
State, Thomas Jefferson, was a lover of France. And because of a slave uprising in Santo Domingo, a large number of French planters had taken refuge in the United
States, where they were liked. Moreover, the man in the
street knew, everybody knew, that France had saved our
life with her army and navy in 1781. Without France we
would have been obliged to settle for something less than
complete independence.

We still owed France many millions of dollars; but we
owed her a great deal more than that—we owed her a
moral debt of gratitude.

The French Revolution was something of a fad, a vogue,
in this country. Liberty poles were erected, or old ones re-
furbished. Liberty caps were worn. The tricolor was every-

where. People saluted one another as "Citizen" or even "Citizeness." People practiced singing the "*Ça ira.*"

It was known well in advance that Genêt was preparing to come, and this knowledge caused worriment in Philadelphia, the capital, where Washington called more than one special meeting of the cabinet.

The cabinet then was not large. Besides Thomas Jefferson it included Alexander Hamilton as Secretary of the Treasury, Henry Knox as Secretary of War, and Edmund Randolph as Attorney General. In other words, there were four votes, and, as Jefferson wrote to his friend James Madison, "Our votes are usually 2½ against 1½," the off-and-onner being Randolph. John Adams was Vice-President, and it may be assumed that he would have made the odds even greater against Jefferson. However at that time it was not the custom for a Vice-President to sit in on cabinet meetings.

Yet if the cabinet was small, its sessions often were stormy. Washington tried to be impartial. Knox and Randolph took now this side, now that. The real gladiators were Hamilton and Jefferson.

Their conflict, a classic, has persisted to this day.

Jefferson was determinedly the democrat. Hamilton had married money and was fiercely aristocratic in his ideas.

They were even a contrast in their respective appearances, these two young men, Jefferson being tall, gangling, sloppy of dress, shy of manner, whereas Hamilton was short, dapper, aggressive.

In Philadelphia, in April of 1793, these two were at it again.

The cabinet was in agreement that everything possible

should be done to keep America out of the new war. We were deeply in debt, and the scars of our own Revolution had by no means healed.

It was more or less believed, too, that France would not ask us to join her, since we would be of more use as a biased neutral; but would not that offend England to the point where she, would declare war against us? Hamilton thought it would; Jefferson disagreed.

As Jefferson saw it, our obligation was clear. We had made the treaty of 1778 in good faith, and made it not with Louis XVI but with France. If the French had subsequently decided upon a totally different type of government, why, that was their business. Hamilton contended that we had made a contract with "the Crown of France," which no longer existed. He also pointed out that the treaty obliged one party to help the other when either had been attacked. France had not been attacked, Hamilton said. *She* had declared war against Great Britain, Spain, and the Netherlands, not *they* against *her*. "Self-preservation is the first duty of a nation," averred Alexander Hamilton; but Thomas Jefferson, who feared that an offended France would turn snarling upon her former ally, warned that "an injured friend is the bitterest of foes."

Immediately there were two points to be decided:

(1) Should this lad Genêt, this new minister, when he landed in America, be received officially, thereby implying recognition of and even approval of the regicides of Paris?

(2) Should Washington, as he wished to do, issue a proclamation of neutrality?

It was at last decided that Genêt should be received,

yes, but in an atmosphere of the most formal and most frigid politeness.

The proposed proclamation of neutrality brought about a much longer debate, Hamilton being for it, Jefferson against.

Jefferson reminded the members of the cabinet that the Constitution gave Congress the right to declare war. Implicit in that, he argued, was the right to declare neutrality. Weren't they the same thing? Only Congress could act on such a question; and the thing to do was either call a special session of Congress—which everyone knew Jefferson could control—or else put the whole matter aside until the regular session reconvened in a few months.

The declaration of neutrality was issued April 22. In deference to Jefferson's feelings the word "neutrality" did not appear in it, but the meaning was plain.

Edmond Charles Genêt had landed at Charleston, South Carolina, April 8.

Why Charleston? Philadelphia, where the government sat, was as near to France and just as good a harbor. Genêt himself said that contrary winds were accountable, but no one believed this. The probable reason was that Charleston as the southernmost large port in the United States, and therefore the nearest to Santo Domingo, contained a large percentage of French refugees.

Genêt was tumultuously received. They went mad about him, wining and dining him, cheering and toasting and serenading him, clamoring that he speak—a demand from which he made no demur.

He had dark, deep-set, expressive eyes. His passionate

belief in his own cause was apparent in everything he did and said.

He had come in a French frigate, *l'Embuscade,* but after a few days in South Carolina he sent her on ahead to Philadelphia. This was even more astonishing. In those days anybody who possibly could do so travelled by water rather than by land. Land travel was back-breaking, heart-breaking. But the ineffable Citizen Genêt did not appear to mind.

He stayed eleven days in Charleston, where Governor Moultrie, among others, fairly fawned on him. He exhorted. He waved the tricolor. He shouted defiance to all tyrants. Also, he set up the local French consulate as a vice-admiralty court with orders to libel and to condemn prizes brought in by French privateers, and he issued no fewer than four privateering commissions.

There is little doubt that Genêt had the paper authorization to do this. There is a great deal of doubt, though, whether he had the right to do it before he had even presented himself with his credentials to the President of the United States. No matter. Genêt was irrepressible, all action.

He took twenty-eight days to get to Philadelphia, a trip that might have consumed somewhat less than a quarter of that time. But he went a long way around in order to visit every Republican, pro-French community that he could find—to organize clubs, make speeches, and hand out commissions, of which he had three hundred.

Genêt was in Richmond when he heard that President Washington had issued a proclamation of neutrality. It must have been like a blow right between the eyes. Now his dawdling ceased. He was all speed. He even broke an appointment to address a meeting at Fredericksburg. He fairly *flew* to Philadelphia; and he burst upon that capital on May 16, exactly five weeks and three days after landing in America.

12 ☆ HE TALKED TOO MUCH

All that had gone before was as nothing compared to what happened now in Philadelphia. Frenzied, screaming, throwing flowers, a customarily staid citizenry went into hysterics at the sight of the new ambassador.

He started well. Work had piled up before he got there. *L'Embuscade* had captured a couple of English merchantmen on her way to Philadelphia, as she was entitled to do. She had also picked up another, the small *Grange,* not on the high seas but in the territorial waters of the United States—in fact, right in Delaware Bay. The British minister in Philadelphia, George Hammond, immediately protested. As was the custom then, the Secretary of State, Jefferson, referred the complaint to Ternant, the French minister. Ternant pleaded an understandable reluctance to act when his successor was so near at hand. As a result the matter was waiting for Citizen Genêt. He listened to the evidence —and agreed with the British minister. He ordered the commandant of *l'Embuscade* to release *Grange*. This was done.

Genêt's power was great. His "war chest" was tremendous. Nevertheless he began to run short of cash, for he had undertaken a mammoth project. He was not only commissioning all sorts of privateers along the Atlantic Coast, not only making paper advances upon Nova Scotia in hopes of taking over all of Canada, but was actually organizing three armies for the capture of Louisiana and East and West Florida.

True, he had made many of these arrangements before hearing of the President's proclamation of neutrality; but he did not cease such activities even after that, for he considered the proclamation illegal. He declared that everything would be changed when Congress reconvened.

In Philadelphia he promptly issued a commission as major general in the French Army to the frontier hero, George Rogers Clark. Clark was to raise a "Legion of Revolution and Independence of the Mississippi" and lead it down that very river. He was to cooperate with an already organized South Carolina outfit, which would drop down the Tennessee. The target of both was to be New Orleans.

All this required money; and Genêt had been ordered to try and collect the United States' debt to France. He approached the Secretary of the Treasury about this.

Hamilton said no; he could not see the United States spending an unnecessary penny at that time. Besides Hamilton, like all Federalists, hated and feared Citizen Genêt.

The Federalists had reason for their fear. They did not like the quick growth of the new Republican Party, which almost to a man was pro-French, pro-Genêt. All over the country political clubs were springing up, modeled after the political clubs of France. Today these would seem harmless, for they were mostly fireworks; but at that time they appeared sinister to the Federalists. What's more, these clubs kept asking the French minister to address them, and Citizen Genêt was most obliging.

His instructions, his political convictions, his experience at home, and the seeming adoration of the American public, all combined to make Edmond Charles Genêt think that Congress was the real head of this state, and that George Washington was little more than a despot. Genêt himself saw no charm in Washington; and he did not understand that the people, by and large, firmly believed that their President could do no wrong. Genêt was too bumptious, too filled with his own importance, to realize that a new young republic was bound to be touchy about its independence, its dignity as a sovereign state.

Nevertheless he won his first test of strength.

Citoyen Genêt was one of the vessels he had fitted out as privateers in Charleston. A few days after his arrival in Philadelphia she sailed into that port with two prizes. Nobody was quite sure of the status of those prizes, or whether *Citoyen Genêt* should be permitted to stay. And so, nothing was done immediately. (The very fact that this vessel bore the minister's name made the whole thing more dramatic. Another Charleston-French privateer, *Sans Coulotte*, had appeared at Baltimore at almost the same time, and didn't attract anywhere near as much attention.)

However, although most of the mariners on the *Citoyen Genêt* were French, two, Gideon Henfield and John Singletary, were United States citizens. The government contended that they were breaking the law, and arrested them. Genêt, of course, sprang to their defense.

Genêt always stressed the 1778 Treaty of Amity and Commerce, and wisely; for many Americans thought that their masters were taking a rather cavalier view of the treaty, and that France was being bilked. Unfortunately Citizen Genêt insisted upon *his own interpretation* of the treaty, and would not even acknowledge any other. "When treaties speak," he proclaimed, "the agents of nations have but to obey."

Henfield, then, was brought to trial, in July, in the Federal Circuit court at Philadelphia. The judges instructed the jury to find a verdict of guilty, but after being out for two whole days, it found a verdict of not guilty. So Henfield and Singletary were both released, and Genêt crowed like a cock.

He crowed too soon. He did not sense that his personal popularity was based upon the cause for which he stood. And that cause began to slip as the summer wore on.

The revolutionists in France were carrying matters too far. The Girondins, Genêt's party, were out; the slavering Jacobins were in, and heads were falling like peaches from a shaken tree.

The United States was filling with French refugees, most of them from the upper classes, who were bitter about the Revolution and willing to tell stories, which, true or not, were calculated to chill anybody's ardor.

August 1, 1793 the frigates *l'Embuscade* and *Boston*, the latter British, met by prearrangement off Long Branch, New Jersey. This duel had been well advertised, and thousands lined the shore or clung to the rigging of nearby vessels to watch. For two hours they banged away at one another, and then the challenger, Captain Courtney of *Boston,* was killed and the Britisher backed away.

This would seem a boost to French prestige, and for a little while it was. But that same day a whole French fleet filed into New York harbor from the West Indies, and *it* was not a boost. A slatternly and dingy fleet, none of its components resembled the spick-and-span *l'Embuscade.* The truth soon came out. The sailors were on the verge of mutiny. Shore parties were to be avoided. There were few open outrages, but a great deal of petty violence. Genêt, to give him credit, rushed to the scene and did everything he could to quiet the men. Eventually they left, but by that time French stock was low.

Desperate, the cabinet in Philadelphia put the problem of belligerents' rights up to the Supreme Court. The court refused to rule.

The cabinet at last issued "Rules Governing Belligerents" which were supposed to eliminate discrimination between France and Great Britain. Genêt spurned them. French privateers were putting into many American ports —and why not? How could a land that had no navy keep them out?

The validity of these rules, their legality, was questionable. Normally the responsibility for enforcing them would have lain with the Secretary of State, since this was clearly an international matter. However the responsibility was given to the Secretary of the Treasury, on the excuse that the customs houses were the most convenient places of enforcement. Again Thomas Jefferson protested; and again he was brushed aside.

The French minister was guilty of various other indis-
cretions, but the *Little Sarah* incident finally made Washington and the cabinet decide to get rid of Citizen Genêt.

Little Sarah was a Britisher taken by French privateers.
She had been brought into Philadelphia, where she was
being refitted and rearmed. When it was learned that ten
cannons had been added to the four she had carried pre-
viously, and that her name had been changed to *Petite
Democrate*, no one could doubt that she was about to become a French privateer herself. This was too much! Even
if the British minister in Philadelphia hadn't protested
(and he did), the American government would have
done so.

Jefferson himself pleaded with Genêt, and was snubbed.
Genêt would promise nothing, at first. After a while he
seemed to agree—though not in writing—that *Petite Democrate* would not sail for some time. However, *Petite Democrate* did sail, soon afterward, perhaps without Genêt's
knowledge. This did not matter. What did matter was that
Genêt, when asked not to release the vessel, had stormed
that he would go over the head of President Washington
and appeal to the people.

The tale spread, urged on by the Federalists. The Fa-
ther of his Country had been insulted! Thousands fell
away from Citizen Genêt, who blustered in vain. Nobody
could do that to George Washington!

On August 16 a message was sent to the American minister in Paris, demanding Genêt's recall.

The French government acted promptly. They were in
truth delighted because by this time they not only wanted

Genêt's recall—they also wanted his head, literally. They wrote him a blistering letter of rebuke. Then they appointed and sent off his successor, with orders to arrest Genêt and send him back to France.

This, again, was too much. Edmond Charles Genêt might be as Hamilton had said, "a burned-out comet"; but so long as he stood on American soil he was not subject to arrest and deportation by the agents of a foreign power. Genêt himself understood the situation perfectly. He knew that if he went back home he was as good as dead. So he appealed for and was granted permission to stay in America. Then swallowing his equalitarian pride, he married an heiress, Cornelia Tappen Clinton, daughter of the Governor of New York. In 1804 he became an American citizen and never did go back to France. He never went back into politics either.

13 ☆ HOW TO WAGE A NON-WAR

The soldier, the sailor, the marine, each regards times of peace as times of routine preparation; but the privateer, when peace comes, ceases to exist as a privateer. That is why this book is studded with wars.

Ships, however, always must be built and must be manned, so even in peace the privateer was not likely to find himself out of a job. But his life then was by no means as thrilling as it had been in wartime. In truth the privateer left the gambling table for the workbench.

In the first years of its existence the United States of America was granted very little peace to grow on. To be sure the Revolution ended in 1783 and a second major contest with Great Britain broke out in 1812, a span of almost thirty years. But the peace in that period was only nominal, and in fact included two undeclared navy wars.

The Dey of Algiers was a greedy fat potentate, who, like his fellows to the east and the west, made a practice of charging commercial nations a yearly sum for protection against the fast-moving Mediterranean vessels under his command. These, as we have seen, were really privateers, though the rest of the world cursed them as pirates. Officers and crew were efficient rascals. They did not kill their prisoners but sold them into slavery, which was still widely practiced in the Moslem world. Amazingly, the European nations paid. Presumably they thought that paying tribute was less expensive than fighting.

Then shortly after our Revolutionary War, the Dey awoke to the fact that there was a new commercial nation in the world. He asked the United States for a trifling yearly contribution—a mere matter of a few million dollars. This was plain blackmail, and the United States indignantly refused. The Dey's rovers thereupon seized sundry American vessels, clapped the crews into chains, and named a stunning ransom. We paid. We had to. And then as if at a signal every other little bey and dey and sultan in that part of the world held out *his* hand, palm up.

We paid, yes; but we soon started to build a navy.

Standing military forces were repugnant to the American people, and at the end of the Revolution the army had been drastically cut, the navy and marine corps disbanded.

But the French and British, locked in mortal combat, showed little respect for a nation that had no navy, and it soon became apparent that if we wanted any attention at all, if we wanted to uphold even our basic rights, we must appear willing and ready to shoot.

The British Navy was being built up, and as usual needed men desperately. It resorted again and again to the press gang, even stopping our ships at sea and taking off mariners on the excuse that they were deserters from the British Navy.

The French, their commerce swept off the sea, their heads turned by their own high-sounding platitudes about the rights of men, were even more offensive. They depended almost entirely upon privateers, their warships being blockaded in harbors. But their privateers were fierce and unethical; on any pretext at all, or on none, they seized American vessels by the score.

Something had to be done about it.

On March 27, 1794, Congress authorized the construction of six frigates. These were to be first-class vessels, war vessels, the best in the world, though not the largest. No expense was spared. Veteran naval officers, men who would command them later, supervised each step of the construction.

This work was done, still, under the Secretary of War. But on April 30, 1798, Congress created the cabinet office of Secretary of the Navy and on July 11 of that year the marine corps was re-created.

Things moved fast.

On July 7 all treaties with France were declared null and void. On July 9 privateering was authorized. The next day President John Adams was instructed and authorized by Congress to tell commanders of U.S. armed vessels "to subdue, seize and take any armed French vessel or vessels sailing under authority or pretense of authority from the French republic, which shall be found within the jurisdictional limits of the United States or elsewhere upon the high seas."

If that wasn't war, what was it?

In the next two and a half years there were many scrapes between small vessels and at least one frigate duel, but no fleet actions. The French privateers were everywhere, but a privateer is not, ordinarily, much of a prize, and since as we have seen legitimate French commerce had been driven off the sea, American privateers, who were specifically forbidden to attack any nonarmed vessel, found the pickings poor.

There were 365 of these privateers, 129 from New England; over 60 each from New York, Pennsylvania, and Maryland; the rest from the south. Most were in fact letters of marque rather than privateers, and sought to arm themselves for their own protection, not for raiding. There were many single combats on the high seas, most of them between privateers, but none, no matter how fierce, were decisive. The two vessels would hammer away at one another for half an hour, or an hour, or two, and then decide that it wasn't worth the trouble. Neither was looking for a vessel that would be hard to take.

This "war" was, however, excellent practice for our

Quiet and good-natured in private life, Joshua Barney of Baltimore was a fiend in a fight. He quit the Navy for a privateering cruise in the fabulously successful *Rossie*, but went back into the service later.

Battle between the *Chasseur* and a British sloop-of-war. A painting by Thomas Whitcomb.

Another Whitcomb painting of the same fight.

One of the greatest of the privateers, Jonathan Haraden of
Gloucester, Mass.

One of the fiercest of the single combats in the War of 1812, in which the U.S. brig *Chasseur* beat the British schooner *St. Lawrence*. It was also the last such fight. It took place February 26, 1815, more than two months after peace had been declared.

ENGAGEMENT *BETWEEN THE* AMERICAN *PRIVATEER* GENERAL PICKERING, CAPTAIN JONATHAN HARADEN *OF* SALEM *AND THE* BRITISH *PRIVATEER SHIP* ACHILLES, *CAPTAIN* WILLIAMS, FOUGHT *OFF* BILBOA SPAIN, *JUNE 4TH 1780*

CAPTAIN JONATHAN HARADEN
A PATRIOT DISTINGUISHED FOR
HIS DARING, SKILL AND SUCCESS
AS A COMMANDER OF ARMED VESSELS
IN THE WAR FOR AMERICAN INDEPENDENCE
LIVED HERE
DURING THE LATER YEARS OF HIS LIFE.
HE COMMANDED THE MASSACHUSETTS
STATE BRIGANTINE TYRANNICIDE IN 1777-8
AND THE PRIVATEER SHIPS GENERAL PICKERING
IN 1780, AND JULIUS CAESAR IN 1782.
HE DIED HERE NOVEMBER 23D 1803
AGED FIFTY-NINE YEARS

"HE WAS A HERO AMONG HEROES"
AND HIS NAME SHOULD LIVE IN
HONORED AND AFFECTIONATE REMEMBRANCE

PLACED BY THE MASSACHUSETTS SOCIETY
SONS OF THE AMERICAN REVOLUTION
SEPTEMBER 25TH 1903

This tablet depicts the fight between the *General Pickering* and the *Achilles.*

The brig *Rambler* built in 1813, at Medford, Mass., a famous privateering port.

Privateer brig *Grand Turk*, 14 guns, Captain William Hustin, master, saluting the friendly *Marseilles*, 1815.

regular naval officers, most or all of them potential privateers. And when, after it was over, they turned their attention to the Dey of Algiers, there was no question of
the outcome. But there was no privateering in *that* tussle,
which took place entirely in the Mediterranean Sea.

14 ☆ GET OUT THERE FAST!

The United States had been edgy for years, but when war
actually was declared against Great Britain on June 18,
1812, it took almost everybody, here and abroad, by surprise.

The French, themselves at war with Britain, were over-
joyed. The British were dismayed and hurt. They pointed
out that they alone stood between the unspeakable
Bonaparte and the rest of the world. They were fighting
the tyrant single-handed; and now their cousins in the
New World had stabbed them in the back. That's what
they called it—a stab in the back.

The U.S. Army and the U.S. Navy, starved for so many
years by Congress, were woefully unprepared for this
fight. Not so the privateers.

In every seaport they had been making boatyard con-
tracts, buying artillery and timber, and storing supplies.
They had been talking to possible enlistees, preparing
announcements for printing. So much, in privateering,

depends upon speed! The skipper who got a head start was the one most likely to make a fortune.

So the race was on. With the declaration of war a rush for licenses started, and boatyards all up and down the coast in hundreds of big cities and small towns resounded night and day to the rasp of saws, the thud of mallets. Mates feverishly examined small arms and master gunners were seeing to the rudimentary fire precautions in their magazines. Everybody quivered to get out there, and right away, in order to grab vessels before they could arm themselves, before they could be huddled into convoys.

Indeed, the first two prizes taken by American privateers in this war were taken *too* soon, both of them in Chesapeake Bay, within a few hours of one another. *Dash* of Baltimore took the British dispatch schooner *Whiting*, and the 8-gunned *Cora*, also of Baltimore, took a similar vessel, *Bloodhound*. These prizes carried no cargo, but they were small, light, fast, and would themselves have made excellent privateers. However, an admiralty judge at Annapolis decreed that they were not fair game, because at the time they were captured the skippers had not heard that a state of war existed. The judge released them.

Yet the work was of some benefit to the American cause, for the crews of *Bloodhound* and *Whiting*, taken ashore to testify, almost to a man refused to go back aboard their vessels, which were thereafter useless to the British. One of the hands from *Bloodhound* told the Americans that he had not been ashore in nine years. This was not unusual. "Keep the pay, keep the man," was a slogan among British Navy captains. On one pretext or another they often contrived to withhold all cash from the jolly tars, who even then would desert as soon as they got a chance, life in the British Navy being no bed of roses. Those who did desert effectively could do but one thing—sign aboard of some other vessel. The deserter had no money, usually his clothes were rags, he had no friends, and he knew only one way of living. He might curse the sea, and probably did, but he was panicky whenever he got out of sight and sound of it. He could sign aboard a merchantman or a privateer, but he preferred to sign up in the United States Navy. There was a good chance of getting killed in the outnumbered American Navy, but almost no risk of being taken prisoner and shoved back into the British Navy. Then too the British could, by law, hang deserters. The best a retaken man might hope for was to be flogged into insensibility, beaten with a cat-o'-nine-tails until he was a cripple for life or a gibbering idiot, or both. Yes, the U.S. Navy was best. Also, the food was fine. And so was the pay. And—you *got* the pay!

At the beginning of this war the United States Navy consisted of 17 vessels carrying 442 guns and crewed by about 5000 seamen. Only eight of these vessels, however, were in condition to put to sea. There was still a great deal of refitting to be done, and restocking, and they were habitually short-handed, especially after the privateers began to enlist. The American ships-of-war were wonderful ships, as they soon proved, the best in the world; but they couldn't be expected to defeat or even hold off a whole national fleet. The British Navy numbered its vessels in four figures, and at the outbreak of the War of

1812, or very soon thereafter, at least 100 of them were cruising off American shores.

Privateers would not engage warships—certainly not frigates or ships of the line, though they might and occasionally did tangle with a sloop or a dispatch boat. Yet they could cause a lot of trouble, and their very existence did help somewhat to make up for the disparity of numbers between the two sides.

Within two months after the declaration of war there were 150 American privateers on the high seas, and more tumbling out all the time.

Some of the first ones were little better than pilot boats; yet even the midgets, given luck, could bring back prizes early in the war. The *Wily Reynard,* a Boston schooner, mounted only one gun, but she sent in three ships, two brigs, and four schooners, a good bag. The schooner *Fair Trader,* out of Salem, Massachusetts, also had but one gun, and a crew of 25, yet she nailed one ship, one brig, and five schooners before she was finally trapped by a frigate in the Bay of Fundy. *Fame* of Boston too had one gun, and she had a crew of only 20. Moreover, she was old; she had privateered in the Revolution. Still in the course of a fifteen-day cruise *Fame* took five schooners. *Teazer* was yet another cockleshell, mounting two guns, manned by 50 mariners, but before a ship of the line overtook and burned her she had sent in six brigs and six schooners, all but one of which reached port. *Teazer* paid for herself many times over.

The reports of all these doings—and there were many, many more—thrilled those at home who heard them, so that not only mariners but wide-eyed lads from the countryside, from the farms, were striving to get aboard of privateers. Mariners, of course, were preferred; for even though a privateer would sail with many more men than were needed to handle her, prize crews could thin their ranks very rapidly. Still there was usually room for a willing, able-bodied youth.

The privateers had all the men they needed all the time. The reason is obvious—glittering successes were much talked about, failures conveniently forgotten.

From earliest days sailors have been a superstitious lot. Privateering pointed this up. How else but by luck can you account for a well-skippered vessel finding herself one morning a few feet from an enemy frigate while a comparable vessel from the same port romps home with a fortune? On the other hand, that second vessel might find her foot slipping a few miles from her base port on the way back, and be unexpectedly captured, driven by one frigate under the guns of another, say, so that her whole half year's work was wasted. Then all the men would spend the rest of the war in a smelly English jail. That's the way it was.

The famous brig *Yankee* out of Bristol, Rhode Island sailed for the first time early in the War of 1812. She carried 115 men under Captain Oliver Wilson, who was twenty-six years old. (There were many Rhode Island privateers called *Yankee, Yankee Lass, Yankee Hero, Yankee Trader*, etc.) Only a few days out, not far from Halifax, she came rather suddenly—for the weather was thick—upon a huge British ship. Captain Wilson didn't hesitate to attack, despite the difference in size. He sent musketeers up into the tops—muskets in those days would only carry about a hundred yards—and he ran out his guns, fourteen 4- and 6-pounders. The better sailor, he got in close.

The big ship was clumsily handled—*Yankee* could have sailed circles around her—but her guns spoke up soon enough, and kept speaking, despite the fact that the gunners had to work in a hail of musket balls.

From the beginning it was the American's fight, and when *Yankee* sped ahead of her opponent and luffed sharply, so that she could blast a terrific broadside into the other vessel, it was all over. The Britisher's captain already was down, and now her flag came down as well. Wilson sent over his surgeon.

The wounded captain was Henry Gambles, and the ship was *Royal Bounty*, bound from Hull for Prince Edward Island. Wilson sent her back to Bristol with a prize crew. She was a 658-tonner, more than four times the size of *Yankee*. The reason she had not made a better show was that she was scandalously short-handed, having only 25 men.

Royal Bounty, though a splendid prize in herself, gave up no cargo, since she had been in ballast. But on *Yankee's* second cruise, off the coast of Africa, the American privateer took the sloop *Mary Ann*, which was carrying ivory, gold dust, and camwood valued at $28,000. Soon after that, in a brilliant smallboat action on the west coast of Africa, right under the guns (fifty of them!) of Fort Appollonia, she cut out the brig *Fly*, which was found to be loaded with gold dust, ivory, iron, gunpowder, and drygoods to the value of $36,000.

Thereafter *Yankee's* luck was fantastic. She couldn't seem to fail, and she never came close to being caught. She made a total of six long cruises under three different skippers. For the second, after the stunning success of the first, she could have had her pick of just about any man in Rhode Island—or New England, for that matter. For the third she was all but mobbed by eager applicants. But thereafter the mariners began to eye her askance—her luck *couldn't* last, they were telling one another—so that when she was shipping a crew for her sixth cruise she almost had to hit men on the head. Nevertheless the sixth cruise was as profitable as most of the others had been; and after all that peril *Yankee* died, as you might say, in bed.

Her greatest single prize was taken in the course of the fifth cruise, the ship *San José Indiano*, English despite her name, bound from Liverpool for Rio de Janiero. The Britisher, together with her cargo, fetched close to $600,000. Of this the owners got about a quarter of a million. Captain Elisha Snow's share was $15,789, while the two Negro cabin boys, got, respectively $1,121.89 and $738.19.

Her prizes totaled forty—nine ships, twenty-five brigs, five schooners, and a sloop.

In all, it was estimated, *Yankee* destroyed $5,000,000 worth of enemy shipping and supplies, and brought home or sent home booty worth more than $1,000,000.

15 ☆ A QUIET, UNASSUMING FIEND

Joshua Barney was burly. He was a slow-moving, soft-spoken man, yet a fiend in a fight. Also, he was wise. He was wise, that is, not in matters of money—he had no head for figures—but in the ways of the sea.

If any man could make a good thing of privateering, the merchants of Baltimore believed, it would be Joshua Barney. The merchants of Baltimore were absolutely right.

It was July 12, 1812, exactly twenty-four days after the infant nation, United States, had declared war against Great Britain when Joshua Barney dropped down Chesapeake Bay in *Rossie,* to make history. He would have left even earlier if the sheriff hadn't insisted that he pay a $1000 debt before departing on this dangerous voyage.

Rossie was a trim small vessel, carrying a tremendous spread of sail, and fast, her bottom recently coppered. She had ten short 12-pound cannons and three long guns, far-reachers, with a crew of 120, four or five times as many as you would expect to find on such a craft—if you did not happen to know her business.

There had been great privateers in the past; there were

to be a few great ones in the future, the near future; but there was never another Joshua Barney.

He was fifty-three years old, born in Baltimore, and had followed the sea since the age of twelve. Nor had he inherited his high position. As the saying went he had "come up through a hawse hole," not through the owners' office.

In the Revolution he had gone with Esek Hopkins to New Providence (now Nassau), in the Bahamas, on a successful patriot raid in which his behavior won for him a commission in the brand-new United States Navy. He became a lieutenant. Twice captured, he was twice exchanged, though in each case he suffered a spell—the total was five months—in a British prison ship in New York harbor. Such an experience could be hideous, and was, except for the short while when Admiral Byron (the poet's grandfather) happened to be in charge.

After Barney's second exchange there was no place for him in the tiny U.S. Navy, so he took up with an old service friend, Captain Israel Robinson, and they got control of a Baltimore schooner loaded with tobacco consigned to St. Eustatia in the West Indies.

They didn't go far. While still in Chesapeake Bay they were taken by a British privateer, which put them ashore at Cinapuxent and sailed off with the schooner—and the tobacco.

Unchagrined, they tried again, this time with a brig called *Pomona*, which carried 12 cannons and 35 men, and carried also a cargo of tobacco for Bordeaux, France. As had been the case in the schooner, they were equipped as well with a privateer's commission, and they planned, after completing the deal at Bordeaux, to learn what they could pick up on the high seas.

On the way across *Pomona* had a brush with a somewhat heavier British privateer named *Rosebud*. But she did deliver her tobacco, for which a good price was paid, and she did take on more guns and more men, so that she was able to distinguish herself in the field of legalized piracy for some months thereafter, snapping up prize after prize. Eventually she was caught by a warship; and once again Lieutenant Barney was clapped into jail.

This time there would be no exchange. Nor would he remain in America, in New York harbor, as before. A new admiral, a man markedly less humanitarian than Byron, was in charge. He had too many prisoners, more than he could hope to exchange, for the bedraggled Continentals had few or none; so he sent a batch of the officers to England.

There were seventy-one of them, and they were thrust into a hold down near the keel of *Yarmouth*, a singularly malodorous warship. They were well below the water line, in a space 12 by 20 feet, so low that they could not stand upright. There was no light, there was no heat—it was midwinter and a notably rough passage of fifty-three days—and no arrangements had been made for cleaning out the place. Neither were they allowed a surgeon, though eleven of them died. The survivors, Joshua Barney being one, were walking scarecrows for weeks afterward. Slaves were never treated so badly, even in the horrors of the Middle Passage. For slaves, being worth money, were made to exercise.

Nevertheless, after reaching England Lieutenant Barney immediately began to make plans for escape.

He and his fellow officers had been thrown into the strong Old Mill Prison near Plymouth, England. From this, after several unsuccessful attempts, at least one of which landed him in solitary confinement for a month, Joshua Barney did in fact break out—alone, and in broad daylight.

It was an elaborate, carefully concocted plot. He had help, of course. In the yard, while skylarking, he had pretended to sprain his ankle, so that for some days he had hobbled about on crutches, which made him look harmless. He wore a long cloak, down to his heels, concealing the stolen British officer's uniform beneath it. He bribed a guard to turn aside. Then choosing his time well, and aided by a tall friend, he scrambled over a twenty-foot wall. He walked through an outer gate, which stood open, and past a sentry, who saw the uniform and suspected nothing. Twenty minutes later he was in the home of friends, sympathizers with the American cause. Nor had he been missed, yet, at the prison: he had made arrangements for this as well.

That night they smuggled him to the home of an elderly Plymouth clergyman, and three days later, with three other persons, none of whom knew anything about handling boats, and all three of whom were seasick, he started for France in a small fishing smack.

A day and a half out they were hailed by a suspicious British privateer. The skipper did not believe Barney's story of a secret mission to France (he was still wearing the officer's uniform) and took the group back to Plymouth, meaning to report them to the admiral. Again Barney escaped, hand-over-handing it down a line suspended from the privateer's stern. By this time the alarm was out, and he was almost captured several times but finally got to France, by way of London, and later still back to America.

There, as though he had not seen enough action in this revolution, he covered himself with glory as skipper of the *Hyder Ally*. Then he rejoined the regular Navy as a captain, in command of his own prize, *General Monk*, the name of which was changed back to *General Washington*.

Here, then, was the man who sailed down Chesapeake Bay so early in the War of 1812: Joshua Barney, quiet, unassuming, and determined. He had been in his twenties when he broke out of the Old Mill Prison; he was in his fifties now, but he was every bit as bold—and as lucky.

He came back in ninety days, in itself something of a record. The *Rossie* had taken four ships, eight brigs, three schooners, and three sloops, with a total value of about $1,500,000.

This haul did not compare with the one *Yankee* was to ring up, but it was easily the biggest on record at that time, and it was made in the course of one short voyage, whereas *Yankee* was to take six.

These prizes had not fallen like plums into Captain Barney's lap. He'd had to fight, sometimes. The privateer *Jeannie* had given him a hot few hours on August 9, as had the British government packet *Princess Amelia* on a certain bright moonlit night, the night of September 15-

16. But he was intact, as was *Rossie,* which bulged with spoil.

Once again Joshua Barney was a hero. His debts would be forgotten. He was offered all sorts of privateer commands. He could name his own terms. But—he said no.

He was, be it repeated, wise.

A million and a half dollars looks large on paper. It is a handy sum to toss around, in conversation. But seven of the prizes had been burned, and others had failed to reach port. Nobody was willing to give anything for the 217 prisoners, though in the Navy these would have brought rewards. There were all sorts of taxes to be paid, and fees, all sorts of forms to be filled out as well. Why, the lawyers' bills alone were piled nigh as high as the loot! The government, too, had to be paid customs charges on all those goods. It was enormously complicated, it was exasperating, it was expensive, and Joshua Barney, solvent now, had had enough of it.

He went back to the regular Navy.

16 ☆ IF A MAN COWARD . . .

Yes, a privateer needed a certain amount of nautical knowledge if he was going to get anywhere, and the more he had the better, for he might be called upon at any time to man a prize and, with a mere handful of his fellow privateers, take it into a distant port. There might be but five or six of them—and fifty or sixty prisoners below hatches. Those on deck would have to do a little of everything throughout the month or more it might take them to reach port, if they ever did. They'd need to handle the helm and handle sail, swab, cook, keep watch, everything, with all the while the fear of an uprising at their very elbows and an unseen enemy just over the horizon. They didn't get much chance to sleep on those runs. A privateer had to be hardy.

It stands to reason that he had to be physically brave. He had been picked for that purpose. As much as possible the average privateering skipper avoided fighting, which was expensive and even dangerous. Fighting brought no glory—only sabre cuts, only bullets. But the skipper was not always given a choice. He might be trapped and have to fight his way out. Trapping a privateer, driving him into a corner, was one of the favorite pastimes of the Royal Navy, often in co-operation with privateers on their own side.

Then there was always the threat of the prisoners, who might break out from below, whether you were on your own vessel or on a prize. *You* and a few others had to handle the vessel. *They* had nothing to do but watch you, marking your habits, your condition. They had nothing else to think about except how wonderful it would be to jump you some time when your back was turned. Of course this called for courage.

There are no records of deaths at sea among the privateers, but it is possible to assume that these were at least as many as in the regular Navy.

There was yet another hazard, seldom faced by the Navy man or the merchant sailor. Privateering vessels almost invariably were oversparred; their sticks, their masts, were too tall, their booms too long. Nor were their hulls, as a rule, capable of taking much of a pounding. In a profession in which your very life might depend upon speed, the privateers spread much too much canvas. They knew this, themselves. It was a calculated risk. Now and then a privateer would crack her sticks and broach-to, dead-eyes under, and capsize. Now and then, too, one would disappear entirely, without trace. That happened down in the West Indies to the *Arrow* brig, skippered by Captain Conkling, with 14 guns and 150 men, no scrap of which ever was seen again; it was supposed that she vanished in a white squall. *Arrow* was not the only one, just the largest.

Yet if there was one quality that was needed above all others, above skill, endurance, courage, it was *alertness*. The privateer as he went about his business must have been the most *wide awake* man in the world.

Just getting out of port in the first place often called for the keenest vigilance. In the beginning of the war Britain had only enough warships to blockade effectively the southern ports, up to and including Baltimore, always a great privateering center. Gradually, however, she extended this blockade as far as New York, and eventually it even included the New England ports. They had been spared until that time because New England was notoriously opposed to the war and was threatening to break off from the rest of the states—something that Old England would have loved. Now, privateers laughed at the blockade, but they did not laugh lightly or for very long. They had to keep their wits about them. One touch of overconfidence when he was sneaking out—or sneaking back—and a man might (as the old-time sailors used to put it) "wake up with sand in his ears" at the bottom of the sea.

The ocean was crowded in those days, yet running lights were not the rule, so dawn after a dark night often found a privateer within a few hundred yards of an enemy frigate, too late to escape. That happened all the time.

In the same way it happened with rifts in a fog. On August 5, 1812, off Cape Sable, the privateering brig *Curlew*, out of Boston, abruptly found herself almost in collision with the overtowering British frigate *Acasta*. The fog, which had muffled all sound, swallowing it, closed in again; but it was too late; *Curlew* had been taken.

At such times, however, minutes, even seconds, could be made to count. For every capture made in this fashion there were a dozen escapes, all close, and all, probably, the result of sharp eyes, sharp ears, and quick thinking. Even in daylight this was true. The seamen were encouraged to keep watching, to keep their eyes peeled, all the time. For this reason rewards often were offered to those who first spotted a sail, as you will see in the articles of agreement below.

Sets of these articles were, of course, filed with the admiralty clerk before each cruise, against the event of a dispute about the share-out afterward. There are plenty of them still available, still on record. This one happens to be that of the *Yankee* mentioned in the preceding chapter. It was for her first cruise, but it is unlikely that the

others were any different, this one having worked so well!
It is printed here because it is typical.

*Articles of Agreement Between the Owners, Officers and
Company of the Private Armed Vessel of War, "Yankee"*

"1st. It is agreed by the parties that the Owners fit the
Vessel for sea and provide her with great guns, small
arms, powder, shot and all other warlike stores, also with
suitable medicines and every other thing necessary for
such a vessel and her cruise for all of which no deduction
is to be made from the shares, for which the Owners or
their substitutes shall receive or draw One Half the nett
proceeds of all such Prizes or prize as may be taken, and
the other half shall be the property of the Vessel's Company to be divided in proportions as mentioned in the
15th article, except the cabin-stores and furniture which
belong to the Captain.

"2d. That for preserving due decorum on board said
vessel, no man is to quit or go out of her on board any
other vessel, or on shore without having first obtained
leave of the Commanding officer on board, under the
penalty of such punishment or fine as shall be decreed by
the Captain and Officers.

"3d. That the Cruise shall be where the Owners or the
major part of them shall direct.

"4th. If any person shall be found a RINGLEADER
of any Mutiny, or causing disturbance, or refuse to obey
the Captain, or any Officer, behave with Cowardice, or get
drunk in time of action, he or they shall forfeit his or their

shares of any dividend, or be otherwise punished at the discretion of the Captain and Officers.

"5th. If any person shall steal or convert to his own use any part of a prize or prizes, or be found pilfering any money or other things belonging to this Vessel, her Officers, or Company, and be thereof convicted by her Officers, he shall be punished and forfeit as aforesaid.

"6th. That whoever first spies a prize or sail, that proves worth 100 Dollars a share, shall receive Fifty Dollars from the gross sum; and if orders are given for boarding, the first man on the deck of the Enemy shall receive Half a share to be deducted from the gross sum of prize-money.

"7th. That if any one of the said Company shall in time of action lose an eye or a joint, he shall receive Fifty Dollars, and if he lose a leg or an arm, he shall receive Three Hundred Dollars to be deducted out of the Gross sum of Prize-money.

"8th. That if any of said Company shall strike or assault any male prisoner, or rudely treat any female prisoner, he shall be punished or fined as the Officers shall decree.

"9th. That if any of the said Company shall die or be killed in the voyage, and any prizes be taken before or during the action in which he is so killed, his share or shares shall be paid to his legal representatives.

"10th. That whoever deserts the said Vessel, within the time hereinafter mentioned, shall forfeit his Prize-money to the Owners and Company of the said Vessel, his debts to any person on board being first paid out of it, provided it does not amount to one half the same.

"11th. That on the death of the Captain, the command

to devolve on the next in command and so in rotation.

"12th.   That no one of said company shall sell any more than one half his share or right of claim thereto of any prize previous to her being taken.

"13th.   That the Captain and Officers shall appoint an agent of said Vessel's company for and during the term of the said cruise.

"14th.   That all and everyone of said Company do agree to serve on board of said Vessel for the term of four months, conformable with the terms herein mentioned, beginning the said term at the time of her departure from the harbour of Bristol.

"15th.   That One Half of the Nett proceeds of all prizes taken by the said Vessel which is appropriated to the Vessel's Company shall be divided among them in the following manner (viz) To the Captain sixteen Shares and all such privileges and freedoms as are allowed to the Captains of Private armed Vessels of War from this port. To the First Lieutenant nine Shares. To the 2d and 3d Lieutenants and Surgeon eight Shares each. Prize masters and Master's Mate and Captain of Marines six Shares each; Carpenter, Boatswain and Gunner four Shares each. The residue to be divided among the Company in equal Shares excepting Landsmen or raw hands who draw one and one half shares each, and boys who draw one Share each. Ten Shares to be reserved to the order of the Captain to be distributed by him to such as he may deem deserving among the Vessel's Company."

17 ☆ THE BEAUTIFUL VESSELS

A few days after the declaration of war the U.S. frigate *Constitution* left Washington, her captain, Isaac Hull, having orders to join Commodore Rodgers and his handful of other American frigates in New York. Actually, Rodgers, fearing some no-action order, had led his frigates out to the open seas on the very day that he got word of war, but they didn't know that yet in Washington.

Hull had to stop awhile at Annapolis for supplies and equipment, and it was July 12, 1812 before he passed between the capes, Henry and Charles, that mark the entrance of Chesapeake Bay.

What little wind there was blew dead against him, from the north, and he had to tack, making very poor time.

At two o'clock in the afternoon of July 17 he sighted four sails to the northwest, and a little later a fifth, making toward shore. This was off a flat sandy island on the lower part of the New Jersey coast—today it is called Atlantic City.

Hull assumed that this was Rodgers' fleet, but he took no chances. He ran out his guns, brought up his balls and

106

powder and sent all men to battle stations. No shots were exchanged that evening. But the others were plainly striving to reach *Constitution,* and with the dawn, indeed, Hull found himself virtually surrounded by them, though still out of range. He was sure now that they were not Rodgers' fleet but British, and he was right. One was a ship of the line, the 64-gun *Africa,* and the others were frigates: *Guerrière, Shannon, Belvidera,* and *Aeolus.* Now, *Constitution* probably could have whipped any one of the frigates, for she was a sturdily built vessel, like all the American frigates, and well handled too. And in truth she *did* whip *Guerrière* a few weeks after this in more northerly waters, when she won her nickname of "Old Ironsides." Against a whole fleet, however, she would be lost. She hoisted her colors, and "ran."

The term is a technical one. In point of fact, *Constitution* could barely *creep* through the water, inch by agonizing inch, so light was the air. And the five British vessels crawled after her, one or another of them now and then getting close enough for a few shots, which still fell short.

Captain Hull played every trick in his nautical bag. He had, of course, cleared for action at the first alarm, and now all messes were cancelled, everybody being at battle stations day and night.

The ship's boats were put overside and men were set to work rowing, pulling. This did not help much, but it might enable *Constitution* to catch a stray fragment of breeze when inches counted. The British, of course, were doing the same thing.

Two 24-pounders were mounted on *Constitution*'s afterdeck, where the taffrail was axed away to make room for their barrels. Two others were thrust through stern windows below. Of the vessels they menaced at too-long range, *Shannon* was the nearest—and she seemed to be gaining. For a British vessel of war *Shannon* was exceptionally fast. And in the United States Navy *Constitution* was rated as slow. If the one could overhaul the other, the resulting action would hold up both of them until the rest of the fleet closed in, and *Constitution* would be crushed.

There were strained eyes aboard of *Constitution*, eyes that were red from lack of sleep.

Captain Hull did not throw any guns overboard, as a privateer would have done, for he might need them in a death struggle, but he did cause 2300 gallons of drinking water to be pumped into the Atlantic Ocean. This lightened ship, a little. It was not pumped directly into the sea but by way of the sails, every one of which was wetted again and again, to close the texture of the canvas.

In those days a frigate would carry six or seven tenders, gigs, Moses boats, and long boats; a ship of the line, a few more than that. The British admiral now ordered all the boats engaged in frantically pulling *Guerrière*, *Africa*, *Belvidera*, and *Aeolus* to go to the aid of *Shannon*. This veritable flotilla soon began to make itself felt.

Shannon drew nearer . . . and nearer. . . .

For this purpose, and with this towage, she furled the sails that would have held her back. But Hull kept his own sails spread, still praying for a breath of breeze. He did get one, for a short time, and pulled handsomely ahead; but then it died, and the canvas hung slack again, so that the British frigate came on . . . and on. . . .

Hull's first lieutenant, Charles Morris, had a thought now. They sounded and found only twenty-five fathoms and a sandy bottom. So they sent out a launch, with a ketch anchor and line. This anchor was dropped about one mile ahead of *Constitution*, and men were put to walking the capstan around, hauling the vessel up to it, a process known as "kedging." Here was backbreaking work, as was the pumping of water and the rowing, but not a man was allowed even a rest, much less any sleep.

Constitution began to outstep *Shannon*.

At first the British could not see past *Constitution* and did not understand what was happening. They were losing the race, but why? When they did understand they were prompt to imitate, and indeed Captain Byron of *Belvidera* even invented a new method of kedging with two anchors, one at each end of a very long cable, so that he did not have to waste time sending one ahead while his vessel stood still. But it was too late. *Constitution* had won.

For sixty solid hours her men had toiled without pause. Now at last there was a breeze, and many of the crew were permitted to drop in their tracks, exhausted. A day later *Constitution* was in New York harbor, the baffled British having been left far behind.

This chase up the New Jersey coast caused a great stir. It was a fitting way to start a naval war largely made up of chases. The privateers, in particular, spent a great deal of their time going after somebody or running away from somebody. They were ready at any time to use the same techniques employed by *Constitution* in that first classic chase, and on occasion they might even develop a few new tricks. A privateer was nothing if not ingenious.

Ordinarily an American privateer had no difficulty pulling away from any British vessel, but he never could be sure what might come into sight on the horizon ahead. There was always the chance that he must sail straight before the wind with a heavily canvased warship at his heels. At such times he might well be overtaken. The chases usually were short, but some of them were long, for time meant nothing to the warships. They would hang on as long as they could keep the hated privateer in sight. One chase on record lasted for eleven days, half way across the Atlantic, and ended with the privateer, which had thrown away her guns, being seized.

Speed was taken for granted. It was at this time that one of the greatest of American developments, the clipper ship, got its start. The idea of slim bows, straight lines, shallow draft, a long stern overhang, came, it would appear, from the West Indies by way of Bermuda. But it was in the Chesapeake Bay district, and especially at Baltimore, that they first received the treatment leading to the clipper.

Flexibility was equally important. A privateer might at any time be called upon to claw off a lee shore, to duck and twist like an open-field football runner, to spin about almost on her own keel. The world never had seen anything like the American privateers of the War of 1812, the wonders of the sea, the amazement of all who beheld them. These vessels must have been mighty uncomfortable to live in, crowded as they always were. The forecastle, with those narrow bows, would be badly cramped at all times and, because of its low deck line and slight beam, would be wet even in a slightly heavy sea. Nevertheless they were beautiful to look at.

The beauty was by chance, a lucky accident. Privateers were not built with appearance in mind, but only for immediate hard use. And there was never the time, even if there had been the inclination, to decorate them with the figureheads, spiral mouldings, raised trim, carved transoms, gilded and filigreed stern castles, and headrails so dear to the slow sailor's heart.

In the beginning of this war a motley cloud of privateering ships and boats had poured forth from all the ports on the seacoast, most of them being small, little more than pilot boats in which a gun or two had been mounted. But as the British developed the convoy system and their single vessels went more heavily armed and manned, and after the first quick pickings in the West Indies had been protected or removed, so that privateers had to cross the sea to find prizes, bigger, better, stronger, and much faster boats were built. These were not converted merchantmen, as had hitherto been the rule. They were designed as privateers; they were meant to be privateers when they were laid down. There was nothing makeshift about them. They were, indeed, wondrously efficient. *Herald* of Salem, *Chasseur* of Baltimore (sometimes called the loveliest vessel ever built), *Prince de Neufchâtel:* these were formidable fighters, not afraid of any vessel, even war vessels, excepting the mighty frigates and ships of the line. They were lean, low, and very strong.

Nor was it the canvas alone that made them so beautiful. From the beginning the fore-and-aft rig had been favored by Americans, and more and more, thanks to the privateers of the War of 1812, the schooner was coming to be considered a distinctively American craft. Yet no schooner could show as much snowy sail as a full-rigged ship with her broad courses, her topsails and topgallants and skysails, with her stunsails fully spread, and her serried jibs.

Rather, it was the lines—those lean, sleek hull lines that American builders loved. When an American privateer came into port it was as though a bird had lighted upon the water, a bird that was prepared to fly away quite as quickly as it had come. There was that same air of effortlessness, of grace. The men aboard of them would have snorted in derision at the very thought, but undoubtedly there was something *fairylike* about American privateers. But they looked that way to the spectator, not to the prize.

18 ☆ THE PLAYFUL ONES

Mention has been made of the patriotism of American privateers. If this did not flame as high in the War of 1812 as it had in the early part of the Revolution, it nevertheless was a living, ponderable thing, not to be sneered at.

The United States was a much younger nation than Britain or France, and her privateers were ardent. Time after time they tackled war vessels of their own size or even larger, a policy any European privateer would have deemed poor business. And time after time, too, the Americans went out of their way to send back to the federal authorities captured dispatches or prisoners who might be of value to the war effort. They did this even before the government (as we shall see) offered to pay for the prisoners and offered also to pay for any war vessel that had been captured, sunk, or burned. What's more, many times they destroyed vessels after sacking them, rather than risk a prize crew aboard of them when there was little chance that they might make an American port. They did not need to do this. It wasn't required by law, and it took time. But it helped the cause.

Another thing that marked the Americans was their humanity. The French corsairs were a rough lot, and the British were hardly noted for their kindliness to captives, but American privateering skippers went out of their way to be gallant after a fight, behaving on the whole like regular Navy captains who were sure of their positions, their dignity, and felt no need to be gruff. This amazed British Navy officers who fell prisoner to American privateers, and who, it would seem, often expected to be scalped. The letters of marque themselves insisted that all prisoners were to be treated with decency and respect, and virtually all of the articles of agreement had strongly worded reminders of this clause. There was never any prisoner scandal in this war, at least none on the American side.

Yet another characteristic of the Americans was their dash, their playfulness. Except in actual combat they were not likely to be grim. They did not seem to look upon the business in which they were engaged as in any way sordid, and some of them from time to time even treated it as a frolic. Also, it was respectable. As we have already seen the Cabots, the Quincys, the Crowninshields were in it. Captain Nathaniel Silsbee of Salem left the privateer *Herald* for the United States Senate. Some of the most distinguished U.S. Navy captains were or had been skippers of privateering vessels: Truxton, Porter, Biddle, Decatur, Barry, Barney, Rodgers.

The sensational *True-Blooded Yankee* (actually a French-built brig, though she was manned by Americans and had been fitted out by a Rhode Islander, Mr. Preble, then a resident of Paris), thought nothing of holding up a Scottish town to ransom, or stopping for a few days on an Irish island for water and firewood, or sailing right into Dublin harbor to sink a schooner that had eluded her the previous day.

The *Comet* schooner, out of Baltimore, like *Boxer*, like *Swift*, and *America* from Salem, like many another, was impudent, to say the least. These privateers seemed to taunt war vessels by going almost alongside them and then darting away, so confident were they of their own speed. It was as though they were thumbing their noses at the British Navy, which was not amused.

Their very names indicate a waggish mood: *Black Joke, Teazer, Orders in Council, Turn Over, Sturdy Beggar, Saucy Jack, Wild Cat, Macaroni, Right of Search, Impertinent.* Two of the most aptly named were *Scourge* of New York and *Rattlesnake* of Philadelphia, both brigs. These, each boasting a record of prizes in its own right, fell in with one another in the English Channel quite by chance, and for some time cruised in company. They were startlingly successful, making hundreds of prisoners, taking more than forty prizes, and bringing in to their combined owners at least $2,000,000.

It was Captain Thomas Boyle of Baltimore, skipper first of the *Comet* schooner, and later of an equally irreverent vessel, *Chasseur*, who perpetrated the most outrageous jape of the war. Boyle was a sobersided person, to look at. He seemed rather sad. He never raised his voice, except in a storm or during a fight.

One of the causes of this war had been the arrogant British "paper blockades" imposed on large sections of the French coast. To be sure, the French were doing the same thing to the British, even more flagrantly and with less excuse; but we were not at war with the French. A paper blockade was simply a proclamation with no warships to back it up. So one afternoon in the English Channel when he was about to send back a cartel, or paroled prisoner, the sardonic Boyle thought that he would issue a proclamation of his own, a *counter*-proclamation, as it were. He retired to his cabin aboard *Chasseur*, and soon came forth with this masterpiece, which he gave to the cartel, saying that he hoped it would be posted on the bulletin at Lloyd's:

"By Thomas Boyle, Esquire, Commander of the Private Armed Brig *Chasseur*, etc.

PROCLAMATION

"Whereas, It has become customary with the admirals of Great Britain, commanding small forces on the coast of the United States, particularly with Sir John Borlaise

Warren and Sir Alexander Cochrane, to declare all the coast of the said United States in a state of strict and rigorous blockade without possessing the power to justify such a declaration or stationing an adequate force to maintain said blockade;

"I do, therefore, by virtue of the power and authority in me vested (possessing sufficient force), declare all the ports, harbors, bays, creeks, rivers, inlets, outlets, islands, and seacoast of the United Kingdom of Great Britain and Ireland in a state of strict and rigorous blockade.

"And I do further declare that I consider the force under my command adequate to maintain strictly, rigorously, and effectually the said blockade.

"And I do hereby require the respective officers, whether captains, commanders, or commanding officers, under my command, employed or to be employed, on the coasts of England, Ireland, and Scotland, to pay strict attention to the execution of this my proclamation.

"And I do hereby caution and forbid the ships and vessels of all and every nation in amity and peace with the United States from entering or attempting to enter, or from coming or attempting to come out of, any of the said ports, harbors, bays, creeks, rivers, inlets, outlets, islands, or seacoast under any pretense whatsoever. And that no person may plead ignorance of this, my proclamation, I have ordered the same to be made public in England. Given under my hand on board the *Chasseur.*

"Thomas Boyle.

"By command of the commanding officer,

"J. J. Stanbury, secretary."

Whether or not this "proclamation" really was posted at Lloyd's is not known, but undoubtedly the habitués there heard about it and quoted it, while merchants and shippers throughout the kingdom gasped at its effrontery, cursing it. This thing was going too far! Damn it, where was the Navy?

Any pronouncement by Lloyd's was to be taken as seriously as the tablets brought down from Sinai; and in regard to the matter of the American privateers Lloyd's was, unabashedly, worried.

In the first seven months of the war, Lloyd's announced, 500 British merchantmen had been captured. This, naturally, sent prices up: flour was fetching $58 a barrel in London, beef $38, pork $36, planking $72 a thousand feet, which was preposterous. It also sent up the price of insurance. Why, it cost 13 guineas a 100 just to ship something across the Irish Channel, which until this time had been considered an English lake! It cost 35½ per cent of the value of the goods to ship them to Halifax!

The mosquito bites were beginning to hurt.

19 ☆ THE HARDER YOU HIT THEM

Loudest and most pestiferous of all those mosquitoes was the same Thomas Boyle of Baltimore who had issued the blockade "proclamation." That particular gesture was only the climax to a series of irreverent tricks.

Captain Boyle was by no means the only American privateer who again and again moved breathlessly close to British warships almost as though *asking* to be sunk, and then darted away, barely in time. But he was the most notable of them.

Boyle operated off Spain, off South America, Africa, France, and in the West Indies, but his favorite cruising ground was the English Channel, for he believed in the stout fighting motto that the nearer you get to your enemy the harder you can hit him.

His two vessels, *Comet* in the early years of the war, *Chasseur* in the later, were both schooners, and almost unbelievably fast. Of equal importance was their maneuverability, far greater than that of any square-rigged or brig-rigged vessel. Each vessel could do almost anything but turn around in its own length. And on the poop of either of these, giving his orders to the helmsman laconically and in a low voice, Thomas Boyle could play with a hulking warship as a slim, supple toreador plays with a bull. And he did. Repeatedly.

An example:

At daylight of February 6, 1813, while among the West Indies, Boyle in *Comet* sighted two brigs to leeward, and promptly went after them. The first struck without demur. The second showed a little resistance, not much. Neither gave him any trouble or cost him any casualties. However, before the second one had struck, still a third vessel, a man-of-war, hove into sight. By questioning prisoners taken from the first brig, *Alexis,* Captain Boyle learned that this and the other one had been part of a convoy of nine sail that had left Demerara for St. Thomas two days before, their cargo mostly rum and molasses. All the others excepting these two brigs and the warship had made the harbor the previous night. They had stood off and on, waiting for the dawn which, alas, only revealed to them the sight of *Comet* bearing down.

The skipper of the second brig remembered a set of suggestions recently sent out by the British Admiralty to all masters of merchantmen. When taken by an American privateer the merchantman should, before being boarded, "cause their gears, trusses, and halyards to be cut and unrove, and their vessel to be otherwise so disabled as to prevent their being immediately capable of making sail." This the skipper started to do, cutting away his topsail and jib halyards and in general making more of a wreck of his rigging than even *Comet*'s cannonballs had done.

It was now a little after nine o'clock, and the warship was approaching rapidly.

From the schooner Captain Boyle saw what they were up to on the brig, for he had seized those Admiralty "suggestions" from a previous prize. He immediately sent over a boarding crew with extra lines and tackle, and ordered them to work fast.

Then he put about and sailed right toward the oncoming men-of-war.

Oh, he had no thought of fighting her! A long cannon-shot away he began to tantalize her with impudent moves this way and that, now sailing almost across her stern, now all but snapping her bowsprit off. He was saucy about this, and adroit. It was the bullfighter and the bull all over again. Comet was holed more than once in the course of these daring moves, but she was not seriously damaged, and she lost no men. She fired no shots of her own.

This business, infuriating the English vessel (inappropriately named Swaggerer), lasted for nearly two hours. Then Boyle, having seen that the second brig, now repaired, was stepping for freedom with all canvas spread, blithely followed her, leaving a frustrated Swaggerer far, far behind.

Captain Boyle did tangle with a war vessel once, but she was Portuguese, not British. That was outside of Pernambuco, on the coast of Brazil, the night of January 11–12, 1813.

Four vessels had come out of that port late in the afternoon, and Comet, which had been watching for them, immediately gave chase. Catching this little group was not hard for the schooner, but it was a little disconcerting to learn, up close, that one of them was a brig-of-war. The others, obviously merchantmen, though *armed* merchantmen, were two brigs and a ship.

By this time it was dark, but a bright full moon was rising. The war brig hailed the schooner, announcing that she was Portuguese and that she was sending over a boat. She did so. The officer, sure enough, wore a Portuguese uniform, and though he spoke English he was undoubtedly a Latin. He stated that his vessel was escorting these three British merchantmen, which Boyle must leave alone. Boyle retorted that he intended to take them, right now.

The officer pointed out that the merchantmen were armed. Boyle answered tartly that he could see that for himself. He added that Portugal and the United States of America were not at war, that this was the high seas, and that he was a licensed American privateer who had every right to take these British vessels if he could.

The officer seemed nonplussed at this. Probably his captain had been bribed to act as escort to the Britishers until they got well clear of the port. However he said, ominously, that the brig-of-war had a crew of 165 men and mounted twenty 32-pounders.

This was a clear bluff, and Boyle called it, warning that if they got in his way he would blast them.

The officer said he thought he'd better go back aboard the brig-of-war and see his captain for further orders.

He did so; and for a long while nothing happened. The moon rose higher; the night was bright. The four vessels drifted along in something of a huddle, though *Comet* had difficulty keeping back with the others.

At last the Portuguese hailed *Comet* and asked her to

send over a boat. Captain Boyle replied that he would do no such thing. He then proceeded to hail the merchant ship, demanding her surrender. She opened fire—and so did he—and so did everybody.

The smoke was so thick (there was little wind) that all five vessels were soon enveloped. This was fine for the *Comet* gunners, who could shoot almost anywhere and be reasonably sure of hitting an enemy, but it was not so fine for their opponents, who might have fired at one another. The Portuguese vessel fell back. One by one the other vessels surrendered to *Comet*. Boyle did not put prize crews aboard of them because he had to keep all his men with him in case the Portuguese (obviously not sure of how he stood) came up fighting again. This in fact she did, but soon fell back once more.

It had been a confusing donnybrook. Dawn revealed that the merchantmen had been very badly mauled. The Portuguese signalled them to follow him back into port, and, forgetting that they had already struck to the American, they started to obey.

Boyle retook one, a brig, but then he just stood by and watched the others, escorted by the Portuguese, limp back into Pernambuco. Obviously he could not follow them there. He had been pretty badly battered himself and needed to make repairs. Besides, the escaping brig and ship were barely afloat; they would never reach any port in the United States for condemnation. He had the best prize anyway, so he let the others go.

Thomas Boyle made a great deal of money and had a great many fights, not all of them decisive. A running battle of eight hours between *Comet* and the 800-ton, 22-gun

Hibernia, in West Indian waters, ended in a draw. But his most famous duel was against an ex-American privateer.

This was off Havana, February 26, 1815, some twelve miles from land, when *Chasseur* sighted and went after another schooner, which ran.

She was about the size of *Chasseur,* and, unexpectedly, almost as fast. As they were soon to learn, the stranger had indeed been an American privateer, *Atlas,* Captain David Moffat, master. She had been trapped in Ocranoke Inlet, North Carolina, July 12, 1813, and captured by boats from Admiral Cockburn's squadron. Then as so often happened when an American privateer was taken, the British, admiring her speed, converted her into an armed dispatch carrier, in this case changing her name to *St. Lawrence.*

That's what she was doing right now, carrying important dispatches, and that is why her skipper, Lieutenant Henry Cranmer, R.N., ran. Cranmer was not afraid, but he had his orders.

Until *Chasseur* was actually alongside the fugitive none of the Americans suspected that she was anything but an exceptionally fast merchant vessel. Very few men were seen aboard of her. There was no sign of resistance.

Then, knowing that he couldn't get away, Cranmer barked an order. Suddenly *St. Lawrence's* deck swarmed with seamen. To starboard ten gun ports were hoisted up as though at a single movement, and ten cannons rolled. There was a terrific broadside.

Chasseur reeled. But she recovered; and in a few moments her own guns were sounding, while musketeers clambered up the shrouds.

Boyle tried to get close, to board, but *Chasseur* in spite of him surged ahead. Cranmer put up his helm, thinking to wear across the privateer's stern and rake him. Boyle, no fool, sensed this move almost before it was made; and he put up his own helm, which brought back his lead and made them virtually bow-opposite-bow.

So they were running side by side again, only a few yards apart, guns blazing.

It was about twenty minutes to two, and a clear afternoon.

St. Lawrence's mainmast went over. That crippled her, and at last Boyle did manage to close. Cutlasses, pikes, and pistols in their hands, his men swarmed over the starboard gunnels of *St. Lawrence*.

They never needed to use those weapons. The British, their captain down, their guns silent, struck.

Lieutenant Cranmer was painfully but not mortally wounded. Captain Boyle sent him the services of his own surgeon, and the two men had a chat.

St. Lawrence was so badly "chewed up" that she would hardly have been a safe prize, much less a lucrative one; and the nearest United States admiralty court was far away. Thomas Boyle released her, as he released all of her men on parole. He even gave them tar and tow and other gear with which to make temporary repairs, to help them stay afloat until they reached Havana. Cranmer was so touched by this gesture that he insisted upon writing a letter addressed to the commander of any British war vessel that might capture Thomas Boyle, pleading that "His humane and generous treatment of myself, the surviving officers and crew of His Majesty's late schooner *St. Lawrence* . . . entitle him to the indulgence and respect of every British subject."

But neither of these polite and courageous men knew that their battle had been in vain. The war was over. It had in fact been over for more than two months. Peace was signed at The Hague, December 24, 1814.

Lieutenant Cranmer learned this the next day, when he made Havana. Thomas Boyle did not learn it until almost two months later, when, on April 15, he returned to Baltimore, all set to squirm through the blockade—and found that there wasn't any.

Such was war, in those days.

20 ☆ GRAB THE PAYROLL!

Though they favored captured and converted American privateering vessels, as in the case of the *Atlas–St. Lawrence,* the British did not depend upon them exclusively as dispatch boats. They had some fast craft of their own.

These dispatch boats, or packets, could be brigs, sloops, or schooners; they were never square-rigged ships. They were small, of shallow draft. They rode high, for they were not used as transports and did not carry ordinary, heavy cargo.

What they did carry, mostly, were mail and specie. This

made them objects of great interest to the American privateers.

Communications between the admiralty in London and the various naval bases involved in the war with America —Halifax, Bermuda, Jamaica—were slow in the best of circumstances. The interception of official dispatches had a tremendous, if incalculable, effect upon the outcome of the conflict.

But it was not the mail that the privateers were interested in. It was the payroll.

Mail could be and often was thrown overboard at the last minute before capture. Gold bullion, being so much heavier, could not be treated in this fashion.

A dispatch boat generally sailed alone or, at best, with another dispatch boat. It was never in a convoy and never had a war vessel for escort. But though it was expected to show a clean pair of heels to any American war vessel, it was not without defenses of its own. After all, it was an integral part of the British Navy. It was supposed to avoid a fight when possible, yet it had guns and when cornered it was expected to make good use of them.

Thomas Boyle learned this when he took on *Atlas–St. Lawrence.* Captain Richard Moon of Baltimore, in the privateering schooner *Globe,* learned it when he chased the two brigs out of Funchal.

Moon looked into that Maderia Islands roadstead the morning of November 1, 1813, and saw the brigs, *Montague* and *Pelham,* "backing and filling." That is, they had upped anchors but they were not making for the open sea, only standing on and off. Moon believed that they were dispatch boats that had been about to sail until warned by a lookout of the schooner from Baltimore. They didn't want to go out until he went away. Of course he could not go in and get them, for the roadstead was Portuguese territorial waters.

Wily, Moon sailed off, on a southerly course; but as soon as he had dropped the islands from sight astern he made about and sailed back.

It was just as he had expected. The two brigs, believing him gone for good, had sneaked out of Funchal. They were headed west, toward America, and it was too late, now, for them to turn back.

They were fast, were *Pelham* and *Montague,* but not as fast as *Globe,* a prodigy of speed. Before Moon could overtake them, however, darkness and a rain squall intervened, and he lost them.

Convinced by their speed that they were indeed dispatch boats, he believed that they would keep the same course, due west. So he did, too.

With the dawn, sure enough, there they were. Moon ran up the Stars and Stripes and went right for them.

It was 10:15 in the morning before the shooting started. *Montague,* the larger of the two brigs, and the rearmost, opened up with her stern guns, Moon promptly replied with his long tom, mounted amidships. *Globe* also carried eight 9-pounder carronades, four on each side. If the brigs worked together, as they gave every sign of meaning to do, *Globe* would be seriously outgunned. But Moon did not mean to depend upon his guns. He had a large crew, and he planned to board the brigs and take them separately.

Globe was badly battered when at last she came alongside *Montague*. The gunnels squealed together. Led by mates John Harrison and John Smith, the boarders, yelling and holding their weapons high, started to leap from one vessel to the other.

Three only had followed the mates to the deck of *Montague*—they were James Thelis, Joshua Brown, and Richard Blair—when the two vessels began to drift apart.

Nobody knows exactly why, but it was instantly apparent that *Globe* could not close the gap. The schooner no longer had any way on. She had barely been able to reach *Montague*'s side in the first place, for her sails had been cut to ribbons by chain shot. Moreover, at just this time *Pelham* crossed the privateer's bow, raking her terribly, so that she became unmanageable.

The two officers and three seamen thus stranded on an enemy deck did not throw down their weapons and cry for mercy. They fought, and they kept fighting until the last one of them went down under a rain of cutlass blows.

Globe could no longer move, but her guns still worked. *Pelham* had taken up a position on her other side, the starboard side, and was pounding her from there, but *Globe* concentrated on *Montague*, on the men who had just killed Brown and Blair, Thelis and Harrison and Smith. Relentlessly, savagely, she kept up the bombardment at that short distance.

Montague's flag came down. *Montague*'s guns fell silent. Her skipper was dead. Her musketeers dropped their guns and began to throw sacks of mail into the sea.

Desperately wounded, Captain Moon turned his attention to the starboard side, and in a few minutes he had

Pelham helpless, her skipper almost dead, but she wouldn't strike and kept shooting.

Now, however, *Montague* began to fire again, and she ran her flag back up on the stump of her shattered foremast. That flag had not been lowered, but shot down. She had not struck, as Moon believed.

This could not be kept up. All three vessels were in a sinking condition. Captain Moon had sense enough to break off the engagement. *Globe* had been hulled no less than nineteen times "between wind and water," and her gunners—those who were left—had to man the pumps. Her hands rigged jury sails on what remained of masts and booms. And she limped away, making with the trades for Grand Canary. *Pelham* and *Montague*, glad to find themselves still afloat, sailed for Teneriffe, another port in the Canary Islands.

21 ☆ TREASON AND TRIUMPH

The invasion of Canada had proved a costly disaster to the Yankees. On land, one defeat followed another. Recruiting was almost at a standstill, and the government could not raise emergency money. Especially in New England, the richest part of the land, the war was unpopular. There was a great deal of talk, there, of secession, of a separate peace. Several governors refused to allow their militia forces to leave the states, though Congress stormed. And the British army in Canada, as its own leaders admitted, never could have held the field, much less prepare for invasion, except for the wheat shipped and cattle driven across the border from New England and northern New York State.

Then there was the matter of the British grain licenses, of the "semi-American" vessels. It was a privateer that first exposed this scandal, and privateers were a big help in putting it down.

The British maintained a huge army in the Iberian Peninsula—that is, Spain and Portugal—where they fought Napoleon. To keep this army fed they were dependent, in large part, upon shipments of food, chiefly grains, from the United States. When war came this trade ordinarily would have been cut off, but the British had thought of a way to keep it going. At a price, they issued special licenses, protecting the shipment of food to the Peninsula from seizure by British privateers and British war vessels. Of course the acceptance of such a license was in itself an act of treason on the part of any American. But some men will do a great deal for money, and here the price was high. Greed indeed did even more to ruin this unsavory business than the privateers. Payment, in Portugal, was made in cash, and certain British frigate captains, eager to pile up a fortune for themselves before peace came, began to nab the returning "semi-Americans" and lift this money as spoils of war. Those expensive "protection" papers, it developed, protected only on the way *there*, not on the way *back*. It was a regular racket, though legitimate, for a little while; but it soon discouraged the "semi-Americans," and the trade fell off.

Atlas, a 13-gunner out of Philadelphia, David Moffat, master, was one of the first fair-sized American privateers to get out on the high seas after the declaration of war, and the very first vessel that she encountered was one of these same British licenses, an early one, *Tulip*, of New York, with a cargo of 1400 barrels of flour and also much salt beef, earmarked for the British troops in Spain. Moffat, visiting the other skipper, pretended to be a *British* privateer. The other, with a leer, produced his "protection" paper. Moffat at once put a prize crew aboard and sent *Tulip* to Philadelphia. He also reported the incident, and touched off an investigation.

Atlas had a good record. Soon after this she took in mid-Atlantic two British armed merchantmen with rich loads, but not without a fight that shook her badly. Moffat started homeward, for a refitting, with his two prizes in company. At dawn on September 2 there hove into sight on a southerly course a large frigate. As usual, no colors were showing. Moffat took it for granted that this vessel was British. The Americans had so few frigates and the British so many that the sensible thing for the Americans to do, everybody agreed, was to take cover in harbors or up rivers, under the protection of forts. If they ventured forth they would be gobbled up one by one, no matter how valiantly they resisted. So Moffat ran.

He did remark that the pursuing vessel was amazingly fast for a Britisher, but he did not learn until much later that she was in fact the U.S. frigate *Essex* on the first lap of her famous run around Cape Horn. And Captain David

Porter of *Essex* supposed that he had here a British privateer with two prizes, so he pressed the pursuit.

The prizes were slow. The frigate was gaining. In the middle of the afternoon Moffat signalled to his prize crews to separate: each should seek whatever harbor could be found. By this time the frigate had hoisted the Union Jack, and Captain Moffat's fears were confirmed; but this was only a ruse, Porter thinking to lure the "British" privateer under his guns by a display of the British colors. As it happened, all three escaped and each made a separate port in safety. *Essex* continued her glorious way in the general direction of the South Pole, but a great deal of time had been wasted.

After sundry other adventures, *Atlas* holed up in Ocracoke Inlet, North Carolina, where she met *Anaconda*, another busy American privateer that had just suffered from an embarrassing error. Off Cape Cod *Anaconda* had fired a broadside into the U.S. war schooner *Commodore Hull*, seriously wounding her first officer, in the belief that this flagless vessel was British.

Atlas and *Anaconda* were trapped in Ocracoke by a large British fleet, from which boarding parties were sent in for them, taking both, though the men themselves escaped.

One of the largest and most successful of all American privateers in the War of 1812 was the 310-ton *Prince de Neuchâtel*, an hermaphrodite of seventeen guns, not a converted merchantman like most but a vessel specifically designed and built as a privateer. The men of *Prince de Neuchâtel* liked to boast that she had been chased seventeen times and had got away easily each time. The fast frigate *Endymion* caught up to her at last, thanks to a freak of wind. This was off Nantucket Shoals the night of October 11, 1814, and both vessels were obliged to anchor because of the lack of breeze and because of dangerous currents. It was a very dark night. Unwilling to wait until morning, when her forty guns would have put *Prince de Neuchâtel* at her mercy, *Endymion* sent forth five boats, containing 120 men. They attacked the privateer at five different points.

Now *Prince de Neuchâtel* had started that cruise with eighty men, but because she had crewed so many prizes she had only thirty-seven left. Even so, she beat off all five attacks, killed many Britishers, wounded others, and took prisoner thirty unwounded survivors. What's more, she slipped away from the frigate during the night when a breeze sprang up.

There were three *Decatur* privateers in the War of 1812, each named after the war hero later to lose his life in a duel. One, a small schooner, came from Maine; she was captured early in the war. Another, a brig from Newburyport, Massachusetts, was the same vessel that had run away from *Constitution*, dumping her guns as she fled. Later, she was fairly successful, though she was taken at last in the West Indies by the frigate *Surprise*.

The third *Decatur* was a schooner out of Charleston, South Carolina. She was armed with six 12-pounders and one long 18-pounder, and manned by 103 men and boys. She did well for herself, taking several prizes, and on August 15, 1813, early in the morning, she sighted the British war schooner *Dominica* escorting a rich merchantman. Diron, *Decatur*'s skipper, a Frenchman, could have escaped; but he thought that the merchantman was worth a fight—and what a fight it turned out to be!

This was a little south of Bermuda. It was afternoon before the two finally met, and they battled for more than three hours. The Britisher was the more heavily gunned. She held twelve short 12-pounders, two long 6-pounders, one brass 4-pounder, and a short 32-pounder mounted on a swivel. Yet Diron had more men and he thought that he could win if he closed and boarded.

He tried that twice, but was held off. At last he got there, running his bowsprit right across *Dominica's* stern, so that his jib boom pierced the British mainsail. Then the Americans scrambled over that bowsprit.

The hand-to-hand fighting all took place on *Dominica's* rather small deck. Everybody on both vessels was involved, almost 200 men and boys in all, and all sorts of weapons were used. It lasted about twenty minutes, and when it was over the captain of *Dominica*, twenty-five-year-old Lieutenant Barretté, lay dead. And every British officer save one midshipman and the overworked surgeon, either was dead or wounded.

Even then, the British did not really strike. It was American hands that hauled down the Union Jack, the British being too exhausted to stop them. Out of a crew of 88 the British had lost 16 killed and 42 wounded—casualties of almost 70 per cent!

22 ☆ WHEN THE DUST
HAD SETTLED

American writers about the War of 1812 tend to stress its naval features—the frigate duels, the battles of Lake Erie and Lake Champlain, the pressure kept on British commerce by privateers. But at the time most people thought of it as a land war; and on land it went badly for America.

Moreover, it would go even worse in a little while. When Napoleon backed away, outmaneuvered at last, as the allies drew nearer to Paris, it became clear that the war in Europe, the big war, was about to end.

Once the French were crushed, Great Britain would be left with by far the biggest and best army in the world, and she already had the biggest navy. She would not pause to catch her breath; she wouldn't need to. She would turn immediately upon her "rebellious colonies," and she would put a swift and violent finish to this other war, the war in America, the petty one that hitherto she had been fighting almost in an absent-minded manner, with her left hand. That would mean the end of the United States of America.

Of the five sea duels of the War of 1812, four between

frigates, the other between sloops-of-war, the United States had won four. These were sensational, brilliant victories, and they elated the American people, as they puzzled, enraged, and perhaps even frightened the British, who simply could not believe what had happened. But their effect was only psychological, not material. They were glorious, but they made no basic difference in the war.

Even Perry's splendid victory on Lake Erie and Macdonough's on Lake Champlain were negative, not positive, in their results. They did not pave the way for an invasion of Canada, a plan that long before had been rudely frustrated. They did, however, make more difficult the invasion *by Canada* (with aid from home) of the United States.

At the beginning of the war the United States had seven frigates, not all of them in condition to take the high seas, and fifteen armed sloops. The British had more than 800 war vessels, almost 200 of them ships of the line. The weakest could easily have crushed our strongest frigate. It was as simple as that, and no amount of high personal courage could change the figures.

In a few months, then, the inevitable had happened. Every United States vessel of war was either at the bottom of the sea or holed up in some river or bay, outside of which, like so many cats watching a mousehole, an overwhelming British force waited.

The blockade was steadily tightened, from the south northward. This was done systematically, and it was done well. Even New England, at last, was blockaded.

Yet the privateers were thicker and more active than ever. They laughed at the blockade. An example: New

York City not only was a large port but it had a "back door" at the end of Long Island Sound. Almost from the beginning the British Navy had paid it special attention. Yet in the course of the war there were 102 privateers registered by New York, most of which went in and out many times.

All was not well, however. Expenses were mounting. The day was past when any old rusty cannon could be mounted in any old skiff and manned with any sort of pick-up crew, and still show a stunning profit. Like the British, like vultures, the lawyers were closing in. Paperwork too had to be done. The world might gasp at the exploits of the more outstanding American privateers, but the privateers themselves did no gasping. They wept, most of them, when they examined their accounts.

As early as November of 1812 the privateers of New York, in their first show of organization, petitioned Congress for relief. They were being ruined, they declared.

Not only were the British keeping vessels from going *out* of American ports, they were equally and perhaps even more efficiently keeping them from going *back in.* Prize after prize was lost on its way to a home port, where alone it could be libelled and condemned. Of about 2000 prizes taken by American privateers in this war, it has been estimated that at least 750 were recaptured by the British.

Albert Gallatin, Secretary of the Treasury and a man of great influence, advised against granting the privateers' petition. The country couldn't afford it, he said. Congress, awed, acted accordingly. But a little later, when Gallatin had been sent abroad on a peace mission, Congress began to legislate in favor of the poor oppressed privateers.

By an act of March 3, 1813, it offered to pay to any privateer who would "burn, sink or destroy" any armed British vessel half the value of that vessel. The destruction of commerce was one of the most noteworthy functions of the privateers; but until this time, in the United States and in this war, the privateer had had no incentive to destroy other than his own patriotism. And if he thought that there was any chance at all of getting the vessel home he would man her with a prize crew. The word "armed" in that law was not too important. Just about every vessel that took to the high seas out of Great Britain and the various British possessions had some sort of gun, at least after the first few wild weeks.

On August 2 and 3, 1813, in three separate acts, Congress offered a bounty of $25 a prisoner, authorized the Secretary of the Navy to grant pensions to wounded privateers, and reduced by one-third the duties on prize goods, which until then had been charged the usual tariff rates.

Even then privateers wept.

There were in this war 513 registered privateersmen, who took 1345 prizes *that they kept*. It has been estimated that about 300 came back empty-handed—or didn't come back at all.

In short, when the cheering had died and the flag had been lowered, when peace at last had been declared, it was the consensus of those best equipped to know that privateering simply didn't pay. Joshua Barney had been right.

He finished in a blaze of glory—on land! For after he

had renounced privateering to rejoin the Navy he suffered the fate of so many naval captains at that time: there was no vessel for him to command. Instead, he was given charge of a fleet of gunboats.

These gunboats were a heritage from the Jefferson administration. The third president of the United States was unalterably opposed to standing armies and navies, and though the war vessels built under the administration of his predecessor, John Adams, had proved mighty handy against the French and the Barbary corsairs, Jefferson stubbornly refused to spend public money on warships. He did, however, authorize the construction of scores of small gunboats, boats designed only for defense, workable only in shallow, semi-inland waters. These were cheap, true; but they weren't good. In any kind of chop they couldn't shoot even the few small guns that they carried, and a dozen of them together under the best possible conditions would not have been a match for one light British sloop-of-war.

To be sure, a few of them under Lieutenant Thomas ap Catesby Jones did put up a gallant, if doomed, resistance off the southern coast of Louisiana when the British expeditionary force against New Orleans was about to be landed. Other than that, the Jeffersonian gunboats had no history. They were meaningless. When action threatened they always had to run away. This is just what Captain Barney's boys did when Admiral Sir Alexander Cockrane led a large British fleet into Chesapeake Bay. They went as far up the James River as they could, and then they burned their boats in order to keep them from being captured.

They did, though, take off the guns first. The boats were worthless, but not the men. *They* had plenty of fight in them. They hauled those guns overland to Bladensburg, Maryland, where an inept general was organizing a stand against the British army landed under the command of Major General Robert Ross and already marching on Washington.

The story of Bladensburg is not a happy one in American ears. Just about everything that could have been done wrong was done wrong, and the ensuing scuffle was a walkover for the English. The militia ran. The regular army ran. The only ones who did not run were Joshua Barney and his naval gunners. They stuck by their guns, to a man, many of them being bayoneted right there. In the American view it was the only bright spot in the campaign that led to the burning of the capital.

So it was that Joshua Barney, himself wounded, again fell prisoner to the enemy. They treated him better this time. They wined and dined him, praising his conduct.

And so too it was that this involved, unwanted, disagreeable war dragged to an end—which to all intents and purposes was also to be the end of privateering. There was but one land victory for the American side, a smashing one to be sure, at New Orleans, but even this took place two weeks after peace had been declared.

23 ☆ IN BAD REPUTE

At the end of the War of 1812, the end also of the Napoleonic wars and the coming of peace almost everywhere, the world felt that privateering had had its day. There was something old-fashioned about it, something almost medieval. For all the regulations, the posting of bonds, the scrupulous care of prisoners, an air of disrepute still clung to it.

Those who argued in favor of privateering pointed out that it harassed the enemy at the expense of private persons rather than of the government. Its opponents answered that the government was ultimately responsible and had been forced, both here and abroad, to give the privateers subsidies or grants.

The privateers could not be commanded: that was the nut of the trouble. They scattered, they went everywhere, their services were duplicated many times. Not organized, and probably not organizable, they could never be counted upon to perform set services. They took men away from the regular Navy and perhaps from the regular Army. They took away cannon, too. In moments of crisis they clogged the shipyards. As far as commerce destruction was concerned, they were unreliable. Twenty-five to thirty well-armed Navy sloops could have done at least as good a job as the 500-odd American privateers of the war just ended, and they would have been much less expensive.

There was another angle to this old problem, a new angle. Iron ships, steam-driven ships, were coming in. Codgers still denied them a future, shaking their heads, tut-tutting, pooh-poohing; but to most men who thought about the subject at all it was evident that the ugly new vessels—the noisy, dirty, shuddering, uncertain contraptions—eventually would prevail.

Oddly, it was America, the land where the engine-driven boat had been invented, that held out longest in the fated race between sail and steam. America had plenty of timber but very little coal and iron, whereas Great Britain, which backed the steam vessels, had plenty of iron and coal, but because of her desperate shipbuilding in the Napoleonic wars, and also because of previous forest wastage, she was woefully short of timber.

America did wonders with the sailing ship, bringing it as near to perfection as ever it could be, establishing with it records that stand to this day—and will always stand. In the centuries since its misty beginnings the seagoing vessel never had known so many improvements and refinements as it did in the comparatively short period between the War of 1812 and the American Civil War; and a great deal of this was due to the privateers. True, the United States did not do it all single-handed, but she did most of it, and she was the leader, as all the world will acknowledge. Hers was that stunning, that proud and beautiful and doomed product, the clipper ship.

Across all the seas those magnificent vessels skimmed, making the world a smaller place. Behind them, rattling, clanking, polluting the air with the greasy black smoke from their stacks, threshing the water with their ridiculous paddles, limped the steamships. You would say, looking at them, that steam never would catch up with sail, and didn't deserve to.

Machinery costs money, as does metal. A man could not build a steamship, as he could build a sloop, in his own front yard. In a future war could private interests afford to construct big steamships? Even in the war just past it had been established, toward the end, that the converted merchantman was not enough, that expensive vessels had to be specially built for this type of work. Would that not be even truer later on?

It was some time before this argument could be proved, one way or the other, for a battle-scarred civilization had determined to settle down to a long period of peace. Men didn't even want to *think* about privateering.

And indeed, for almost half a century the American people had no occasion to be reminded of the practice, except from time to time through the medium of the long, vexatious, complicated, and in the end unproductive *Armstrong* Claims.

As was so often the case with privateers, the schooner *General Armstrong,* scuttled and burned in Fayal harbor, as described in our first chapter, had many owners. At the end of the war each of these and later their heirs sued the Portuguese government, alleging that it was at fault in letting the British Navy violate its neutrality. Portugal refused to pay unless she could first collect from Great Britain, and Britain stoutly denied that her Navy had done anything wrong.

This wrangle went on for many years, accumulating a great mass of letters, notes, and legal papers, through secretary after secretary, minister after minister, court after court, getting nowhere, until at last all parties agreed upon the Emperor of France, Napoleon III, as arbiter. He decided in favor of Portugal, and nobody paid anybody anything.

(Perhaps in part because of a feeling of guilt, Portugal was later to fish the *General Armstrong*'s swivel gun from the bottom of Fayal harbor and present it to the United States. It was exhibited at the Chicago World's Fair in 1893.)

The United States declaration of war against Mexico in 1846 held no mention of letters of marque and reprisal, and though that provision remained in the Constitution, as it does to this day, nothing was done about it. The reason is simple. Mexico had no sea commerce.

When the Crimean War broke out in 1854 Great Britain flatly—and somewhat unexpectedly—announced that she would not grant letters of marque. No great sacrifice was involved, for it would hardly have been practical for British privateers to harry the few Russian vessels they might happen to meet in the Black Sea, the western Baltic, or the Pacific Ocean. Still the announcement had a ring of finality about it, coming as it did from the world's greatest carrier.

When that particular war was over, in 1856, the participants and a few well-wishers gathered at Paris to make a peace that they earnestly hoped would last. Out of the conference came this "solemn declaration":

"1st. Privateering is and remains abolished;

"2nd. The neutral flag protects the enemy's goods, except contraband of war;

"3rd. Neutral goods, except contraband of war, are not subject to seizure under the enemy's flag;

"4th. Blockades, to be binding, must be effective; i.e., maintained by a force sufficient to render approach to the enemy's coast really dangerous.

"The governments of the undersigned plenipotentiaries engage themselves to bring this declaration to the attention of those States which have not been invited to participate in the Congress of Paris, and to invite them to accede to it.

"Convinced that the maxims which they have proclaimed cannot but be received with gratitude by the whole world, the undersigned plenipotentiaries have no doubt that the efforts of their Governments to make their adoption general will be crowned with full success.

"The present declaration is not and shall not be binding except among the Powers which have signed or may accede to it."

The original signers, the conferees at Paris, were France, Great Britain, Russia, Prussia, Austria, Sardinia, and the Sublime Porte (Turkey).

On the whole, this so-called Declaration of Paris was well and even enthusiastically received as a serious, thoughtful move toward world understanding. Hanover and the Two Sicilys acceded to it right away, followed within only a few months by the Papal States, Electoral Hesse, Tuscany, Belgium, the Netherlands, Olderberg, Saxe-Altenburg, Sweden and Norway, Bremen and the Grand Duchy of Hesse, Saxony, Nassau, Lübeck, Greece, Saxe-Weimer, Saxe-Coburg-Gotha, Denmark, Würtemberg, Bavaria, the German Confederation, Macklenburg-Schwerin, Portugal, Baden, Chile, Parma, Macklenburg-Strelitz, Guatemala, Haiti, the Argentine Confederation, Ecuador, Peru, Brunswick, Brazil, and Switzerland.

Of those asked, the only nations showing a reluctance to accede to the Declaration of Paris were Spain, Mexico, and the United States of America.

Each of these, be it noted, was a country with a long coastline and a weak navy, and Spain especially was doubtful about the free-ships, free-goods clause, her own adherence to the very opposite view being a tradition.

President Pierce of the United States was perplexed. On the one hand, he did not see how with the world the way it was the United States could *afford* just then to foreswear privateering. On the other hand, he was personally, and he knew that the country was generally, in favor of more liberal maritime laws. Also America would not be pleased to find herself in the company of such backward nations as Mexico and Spain as against virtually all the rest of the Western world.

Pierce's answer was sent, naturally, through his Secretary of State, William L. Marcy, a tall, heavy-set man with a leonine head but with a twinkle in his eye. It has gone down in history as the Marcy Amendment, though properly it was no amendment at all but a whole new proposition, the adoption of which would have made all four of the other clauses unnecessary.

The Marcy Amendment said, in diplomatic language: Why not make a definite stand that *all* goods travelling by sea in time of war (excepting contraband) be as safe from seizure as though they were on land?

This was too direct, too plain, too sudden. It went to the heart of the matter, and went there too quickly. Though it was copiously discussed, nothing much else was done about it.

And then along came the American Civil War, and the whole situation was changed.

On April 10, 1861, Fort Sumter in Charleston harbor was called upon to surrender, and on April 13, after a bombardment, it did so.

On April 15 Abraham Lincoln, the newly sworn-in president, issued a call for 42,000 volunteers to serve for three years or as long as the war should last. Nobody, in the North at least, thought that it would last long.

On April 17 Jefferson Davis, president of the just-organized Confederate States of America, issued an invitation for applications for letters of marque—and got a great many answers. Davis did this under the extraordinary war powers granted him by the Confederate Congress, but as a strict constitutionalist he was relieved and pleased when soon afterward that Congress specifically endorsed his action, passing a law to that effect.

It was a come-on law. It called for bonds of $5000 for privateers manned by fewer than 150, $10,000 for those of 150 or more. It stipulated that every application must be backed by a bought, cleared vessel: there would be no blank commissions. And it made it extremely easy for the privateer to collect his prize money.

On April 19 President Lincoln declared the southern states to be in a state of blockade, and the United States Navy went into action. This was to be a real blockade, not a "paper" one.

In answer to Jefferson Davis's call for privateers President Lincoln issued yet another proclamation in which he declared that "such persons [captured privateersmen] will be held amenable to the laws of the United States for the prevention and punishment of piracy." In other words, they would be hanged.

This brought forth a screech of disapproval from the South, and, as the event was to prove, it was ill advised and rash.

One of the first matters the new cabinet at Washington had to face was the unfinished business about the Declaration of Paris. Soon after the Marcy Amendment was sent out President Pierce had been succeeded by President Buchanan, who asked that this amendment be recalled in order to give him time to study it. This was done. Whether or not President Buchanan did study the Amendment and the Declaration of Paris he never did anything about them, and when President Lincoln took office there they still were on the State Department's desk.

They were taken up early, and it seemed to a majority of the cabinet members that they should be acted upon—and immediately. The South had seceded and was calling for privateers. The North, with a huge sea traffic, took that summons seriously. It was decided to accede to the Declaration of Paris right away, with or without the Marcy Amendment. On April 24 a circular dispatch went out to ambassadors and ministers in Belgium, the Netherlands, Denmark, Austria, Prussia, Great Britain, and France, directing them to sound out their various governments.

On May 13 a new ambassador to the Court of St. James, Charles Francis Adams, son of John Quincy Adams, arrived in London with his son and secretary Henry, the future historian. That very day the foreign minister, Lord John Russell, had struck an agreement with the French foreign minister, M. Thouvenel, to issue a proclamation of neutrality, and this they both did the next day, May 14.

In the circumstances a proclamation of neutrality amounted to recognition of the Confederate States of America as a separate, sovereign nation. The United States, understandably, didn't like this, especially as the example was followed by so many other European nations. To the United States this fighting was not properly a war at all but only an uprising, albeit a very large uprising.

Adams did not get an audience with the foreign minister until May 18, and at that time Lord Russell expressed the belief that the matter could be handled better by the British ambassador in Washington dealing directly with the Secretary of State. This was done; but since the British ambassador, Lord Lyons, was not authorized to strike a formal agreement, any more than was the French ambassador, the matter was tossed back into the laps of Paris and London. Adams, together with Dayton, the U.S. ambassador at Paris, distinctly felt that he was being stalled.

He was, and they were. This sudden interest in the

Declaration of Paris on the part of a nation that had not even mentioned the subject for five years, was too obvious. The word "pirate" was not spoken nor written into any official paper, but it hung there, glittering balefully, all the same. Great Britain and the France of Napoleon III had no intention of being obliged to regard possible Confederate privateers as pirates. They pointed to their respective proclamations of neutrality, in which the Confederacy was recognized as a belligerent. They added, under their breath, that the U.S. Senate would never ratify such an arrangement anyway. They did make it clear —and the other European nations echoed them—that no privateers, of either side, would be permitted to use their harbors or facilities. Further than that they would not go.

So it was that the United States never did accede to the Declaration of Paris.

24 ☆ BABIES WERE HELD UP

The South had no maritime tradition. There were not many good harbors there. At the outbreak of war the South owned about one sixth of the nation's shipping, but much of that was tied up in the North, where it was quickly confiscated.

In the War of 1812 when every port from Baltimore north was spewing privateers by the score, Norfolk dispatched only six; Wilmington, North Carolina, three; New Orleans, six; Savannah, five; Charleston, thirteen.

For all the careful wording of the law that authorized it, Confederate privateering was a catch-as-catch-can business. The Southerners were so heavily outnumbered in men, money, and material, that from the beginning it was clear that they must resort to unconventional methods. Their privateering fleet was a motley one.

The first vessel to be commissioned was the *Triton* schooner out of Brunswick, Georgia, which carried 20 men and one 6-pounder swivel gun. The second was *Phenix*, a steamship rated at 1644 tons, carrying 7 guns and 243 men. Neither of these got anywhere.

At New Orleans there was built by private enterprise a steam ram, thus combining one of the oldest and one of the newest of sea-fighting devices. It was designed to pay for itself by sinking the expected invasion vessels, for each of which the Confederate government would pay a bounty. However it never did amount to anything.

It was at New Orleans too that the first privateering submarine was built. Aptly named *Pioneer*, she was a cigar-shaped thing 20 feet long, her greatest inside beam 3 feet, 2 inches. She carried a propeller at each end, one for coming, one for going, and these were turned by two members of the crew of three, who worked a crank. She was fabricated of quarter-inch iron sheets riveted together, and she must have been mighty uncomfortable. Like David Bushnell's *Turtle* in the Revolutionary War, *Pioneer* was not designed to do any real fighting, only to get close to an enemy vessel unseen and fasten an explosive. It did blow up a barge on its tryout in Lake Pontchartrain, but when the submarine was put into the river it sank. *Pioneer* was rated at four tons, and its privateering commission was issued March 31, 1862.

The first prizes taken by the Confederates were captured in the Gulf of Mexico. Three New England whalers, *John Adams, Panama,* and *Mermaid* were seized by *Calhoun,* a converted tow barge out of New Orleans.

Retribution had originally been a Lake Erie tug, with the name *Uncle Ben.* The United States Government converted it into a gunboat, but at the outbreak of war it was seized in southern waters. Then its engine was taken out by the Southerners who rigged it as a schooner. *Retribution* made a good record, as Confederate privateers went.

The tiny *Petrel,* 2 guns, a former revenue cutter, tried to sneak out of Charleston. When chased by the 52-gun U.S. frigate *St. Lawrence* she had the temerity to turn and fight. She was sunk with one broadside.

The Confederates put a great deal of faith in *Rattlesnake,* perhaps because the *Rattlesnake* of the War of 1812 had been successful. No fewer than twenty-seven residents of Charleston invested in this one, a steamship rated at 1220 tons and carrying a crew of 130. But *Rattlesnake II* never did get out of Ogeechee River to the open sea. She was sunk, in November of 1862, by blockading vessels.

Hatteras Inlet, just south of Hatteras Light, soon became a gathering place for the offshore privateers, small vessels that at a signal from the light would leap out, pounce upon some unsuspecting passer, plunder him, and scurry back to cover in a place too shallow for war vessels. The U.S. Navy soon stopped this by plugging the several entrances to the inlet with sunken hulks filled with stone.

All of these events and others like them, however, were as nothing when compared with the consequences of two momentous cruises, those of the *Savannah* and the *Jefferson Davis*.

Savannah was a schooner, a former Charleston pilot boat. Of her twelve owners, two—T. Harrison Baker, a fine figure of a man with a red beard, and John Harleston, twenty-eight years old, a former Texas rancher—went with her as captain and mate respectively. Full of high hope, she headed for Hole-in-the-Wall, the Bahamas. She had but one gun, an old, short 18-pounder mounted on a swivel amidships, a relic of the War of 1812. She had a crew of twenty, including a Chinese cook. They were mostly young men.

She stopped the brig *Joseph*, Rockland, Maine, with a cargo of sugar. She put a prize crew aboard and sent her back to Charleston, where she fetched $30,000. Meanwhile *Savannah* herself was running into hard luck. *Joseph* was not even out of sight when the U.S. brig-of-war *Perry* appeared. *Savannah* ran, but she had lost some of her top hamper in a blow the previous day and she wasn't as fast as usual. Around eight o'clock that evening the brig caught up with her. They could barely see one another.

The brig was flying the Stars and Stripes, and now the schooner gallantly hoisted the Stars and Bars. Both opened fire, each aiming at the other's gun flashes. But *Perry* had six pieces, the privateer only that one old one, so the battle didn't last long. *Savannah* struck her colors, and then, since this might not be seen, struck her sails as well.

The prisoners were transferred to another vessel and sent to New York. Their landing caused vast excitement.

It was a Sunday. The men, handcuffed to one another, were paraded from the Battery to the Tombs through streets black with persons who had turned out to see the "pirates." Babies were held up, so that they too could see.

These men were in fact formally charged with piracy.

Immediately Jefferson Davis took pen in hand, and wrote a letter to President Lincoln himself. Lincoln refused to accept it, but it was opened at last by General Winfield Scott, top-ranking officer in the United States Army. It was explicit:

". . . painful as will be the necessity, this Government will deal out to prisoners held by it the same treatment and the same fate as shall be experienced by those captured on the *Savannah*, and if driven to the terrible necessity of retaliation by your execution of any of the officers or the crew of the *Savannah*, that retaliation will be extended so far as shall be requisite to secure the abandonment of a practice unknown to the warfare of civilized man, and so barbarous as to disgrace the nation which shall be guilty of inaugurating it."

No answer was made to this, but all the world waited to see if Lincoln would back down.

The single privateering cruise of the *Jefferson Davis* was much more eventful. She was a brig owned by eight Charleston men, one of whom, Louis M. Coxetter, a short, plump, gentlemanly personage with a goatee, was her skipper. She carried five iron guns, English, even older than *Savannah*'s one swivel. She was painted black and had dark hempen sails, which must have given her a sinister appearance. She had formerly been a slaver, under the name *Echo*.

Jefferson Davis headed north, and off the coast of Delaware picked up the brig *John Welsh,* heading from Trinidad for Falmouth with a cargo of sugar. Coxetter put a prize crew aboard and sent this back successfully.

Next they stopped a vessel that proved to be British, and Captain Coxetter apologized most profusely.

Jefferson Davis then picked up two small vessels, separately, but let each go as a cartel after each skipper had promised to continue his voyage to South America. Both promises were broken as soon as the Confederate was out of sight, the skippers hurrying home to give the alarm. That part of the ocean soon swarmed with U.S. Navy vessels.

The Confederate privateers next captured the schooner *Enchantress,* July 6, 1861, took off all her men except a Negro cook, Jacob Garrick, and put on a prize crew headed by Willian Smith, a small, dark, heavily bewhiskered man. *Enchantress,* however, never got back to Charleston. Near there she was hailed by the U.S.S. *Albatross,* out of the Philadelphia Navy Yard. All might have been well but for the cook, Garrick, who should have been locked in the forecastle. Instead he was allowed the freedom of his galley. The prize crew answered the hail satisfactorily, posing as the original crew of this harmless vessel, and the *Albatross,* convinced, was turning away— when the cook bounded out on deck, waving his arms and shouting that he was a prisoner and that these men were Confederate privateers. The *Albatross,* understandably, took a better look. All the prize crew were sent to Philadelphia, where (excepting the cook, of course) they were thrown into Mayamensing Prison on a charge of piracy.

Jefferson Davis seemed to have bad luck with her Negro cooks. There was another one aboard her next prize, the schooner *J.S. Waring* out of Brookhaven, Long Island. Again he was left on that vessel, which was staffed with a prize skipper, two prize mates, and two prize seamen, and sent back for Charleston. She, too, never reached Charleston. One fine night, when, apparently, no watch was kept—for the two seamen were in the forecastle, the captain and one mate were asleep in their bunks, and the other mate was snoozing on the poop deck—the cook, a burly man from Rhode Island named Tillman, took an ax and went on the prowl. He cut up the captain, then the first mate, then the second, the one on the poop. He had to hit them quite a few times, a very messy business, and he heaved each one overboard, though it was not certain that they were all dead. After this he did not have to hack the seamen into submission, one sight of that blood-smeared ax being enough. Then, incredibly, Tillman, who knew nothing about navigation, caused the *J.S. Waring* to be turned north, and, staying awake somehow, and being lucky in the weather, he sailed her all the way to Sandy Hook.

His arrival caused a tremendous sensation. The surviving seamen were, of course, arrested as pirates, but Tillman himself was made a great hero, and P. T. Barnum, signed him up for his circus. For several months, then, while suckers gasped, Tillman displayed his toothy grin, his blood-stained ax, and the confiscated Confederate flag.

So now in Philadelphia and New York the federal government had fourteen men taken at sea and charged with piracy. What would be done with them?

25 ☆ END OF AN ERA

Jefferson Davis meant what he said. When the news reached him in Richmond he went into action at once.

The first New York trial had been inconclusive, though attended by much fanfare. An exceptionally intelligent jury was out for twenty hours, only to announce at last that it could not possibly agree. Defense counsel, an impressive array of dramatic talent, some hired by the Confederate States of America, others by local well-wishers, but all acutely aware of the stage upon which they strutted, promptly moved for an immediate second trial. This was denied, and the defendants, still handcuffed, were sent back to the Tombs to await their turn, which would probably not come again for a couple of months. They were treated not like prisoners of war but as common felons. Jefferson Davis found this additionally rankling.

The prize crew of *Enchantress* was tried in Philadelphia. One pleaded not guilty, on the ground that he was out of sympathy with the Southern cause, that he had been forced to serve on the privateer. The case against him was not pressed.

The prize captain, Smith, was tried first. The trial lasted four days, and though it was well attended it was less of a three-ring circus than the one in New York. Smith was found guilty.

Then the other three were tried, and they too were found guilty.

The day after this piece of news was received at Richmond a drawing for hostages was held in the Confederate Provost Marshal's office. President Davis ordered the hostages to be picked according to rank, the highest first. This was still early in the war, so the Confederates had no captive generals and not even enough colonels to go around—only eleven. Seemingly there were no majors at all among the prisoners, for the list was filled out with three captains. The names were put on uniform slips of paper, which were placed in a can. The drawing was done with suitable ceremony, in the presence of sundry Confederate officials and Northern prisoners.

The first name drawn was that of Colonel Corcoran, 89th New York State Militia Regiment. He was, then, hostage for William Smith, who, it was expected, would be the first to go. Corcoran would hang when Smith hanged. Each of the others was then made hostage for a particular privateer prisoner. They were all taken out of military prison and lodged in the public jail, "like common felons," as President Davis had ordered.

That was in October. Not until February did the government at Washington at last give in. Quietly and rather shamefacedly, it sent out orders that the privateers should be given prisoner-of-war status. Eventually they were all exchanged.

This was the last time that anybody took privateering seriously. The South, though more desperate than ever, had already discarded it. The vessels available to the Confederacy were not big enough or strong enough to venture far from home, and the blockade of the Southern states themselves was getting tighter every day. There weren't enough cannons to go around, nor could the privateers restock their supply of artillery from every prize, as privateers had done in previous wars. Such prizes as were sent in were welcome for their cargos, but hardly for themselves. They were slow vessels—they wouldn't have been caught otherwise—and in the grip of that blockade the South needed speed above everything else. Speed indeed was always the privateer's best friend.

The destruction of enemy commerce was important, and the United States was peculiarly susceptible to this, as the Confederacy well realized, but privateers were not the best means. What war vessels the Confederate States Navy did manage to get into the water were devoted to the destruction of commerce. They didn't need to think of the value of a prize or weaken themselves with the appointment of prize crews. They simply sank everything they could. The celebrated killer *Alabama*, for example, was a commissioned C.S.N. vessel, not a privateer.

When what was left of the crew of *Jefferson Davis* got back to Charleston after that one momentous seven-week cruise, the city was wild with its welcome, hailing them as heroes. But in truth there had never been much glitter in privateering; and when the ragged crew of the *Savannah* at last returned, about a year later, it was pity, not adulation, that they inspired. By that time, anyway, privateering had ceased to be, giving way for a short while, until the U.S. Navy pulled its garrot tight, to the blockade runners.

The blockade runners did have glamor, while they lasted. They did not cruise hopefully, like the privateers. The blockade runners rather *darted*, preferably at night. It was a life full of excitement, and rich in profits. Blockade-running skippers were pointed out in the streets as privateer skippers never had been. Rhett Butler of *Gone With the Wind* was a blockade runner, not a privateer.

And so it was that privateering died, ingloriously, even a little ludicrously. It had enjoyed its moments of color, of thrills, even its moments of grandeur; but it was poorly organized, a discontinuous system dependent upon wars, and it had suffered from a bad press. It had no central office, no continuing tradition, no official historian, and as a result amazingly little has been written about it, by Americans at least. In the mind of the average man today it is inextricably entangled with piracy, and indeed many millions must believe that privateering and piracy were one and the same thing.

Yet Americans have no reason to be ashamed of a history of privateering. The Navy might damn it as irresponsible, irregular, and a great waste, and Henry Adams, the historian, might argue that the same amount of money spent on small vessels of war, manned by regular Navy men, subject to Naval orders and Naval discipline, would result in much greater efficiency. For Navy vessels would sink or burn their prizes, not send them back so that they could be recaptured, as happened so many times with privateers. Nevertheless privateering was a system peculiarly adapted to a young, growing, hardy, maritime nation.

The privateer needed, above all, independence, initiative, imagination. He was on his own. He could not "go by the book."

Independence, initiative, imagination—these are markedly American characteristics. And so it is no wonder that this nation took to privateering early, played it harder and faster in proportion to population than did any other seagoing country, and was the very last to lay privateering aside when clearly it had outlived its usefulness.

Independence, initiative, imagination: applied to privateering, together with a liberal dash of courage, these have resulted in some of the most stirring pages of American history, pages of which we should always be proud.

☆ GLOSSARY

BARNACLE. It looks like an oversized, very dirty oyster. By means of a long fleshy foot-stalk it attaches itself to the bottoms of vessels at sea. This cuts speed; and privateers, dependent as they were on speed, had to have their bottoms scraped more often than most other vessels.

BINNACLE. The box, usually round and about waist-high, in which the compass is kept. It used to be called the BITTACLE.

BITTACLE. See BINNACLE.

CLAW OFF A LEE SHORE, TO. Square-rigged vessels, which could only sail about 90 degrees into the wind, had a hard time of it when that wind was squarely abeam and pushing them toward a beach. They had to make a series of clumsy yaws or tacks. This was known as clawing off a lee shore, and it was a delicate and dangerous operation. Fore-and-aft-rigged vessels, such as schooners, could sail about 45 degrees into the wind. This gave them a substantial advantage over the square-rigged vessels off a lee shore, in the event of a chase.

COUNTERSCARP. A fortifications term. The counterscarp was the wall on the enemy side of a ditch or moat surrounding a fort. The wall on the fort side, part of the rampart proper, was the SCARP.

COVERED WAY. A narrow walk along the top of the COUNTER-SCARP. It was lower than the SCARP, so that the fort's cannons shot over the heads of musketeers or grenadiers stationed there to check the first rush of the enemy. These men were protected by an earthwork.

DONNYBROOK. A brawl. A free-for-all fight. It was named after the Donnybrook Fair in Ireland, which used to be notorious for its every-man-for-himself fist battles.

FALLING OFF. Turning a vessel downwind, in order to run.

FLECHE. In French this means "arrow." In siegecraft it was a small earthwork shaped like the head of an arrow and open in the rear.

FORECASTLE. Pronounced "f'c'sul" in two syllables, and sometimes spelled FOCSUL. The earliest oceangoing vessels (not counting those of the Vikings) were protected by two high fighting towers. The one in the bow was called the forward or forecastle, the one in the stern was the AFTER CASTLE. Traditionally the FORECASTLE was the sleeping quarters of the crew, while the officers were berthed in the stern, the AFTERDECK or POOP or QUARTERDECK being the place from which the vessel was controlled, since it contained the helm. The FORECASTLE was an uncomfortable place, especially on clipper ships with their narrow bows. Today ordinary and able-bodied seamen are usually berthed amidships, but their quarters are still called the FORECASTLE.

GUINEAMAN. A slave ship. Most of the slaves taken to the West Indies and to continental America came from the Guinea coast of Africa. The vessels that carried them were highly malodorous, and "stinks like a Guineaman" or "stinks like a slaver" were common expressions of the time.

GUNNELS. The word was originally GUNWALLS, and that's just what they were—stout wooden walls that ran around the upper deck or decks to protect the guns and the gunners there. Today we call this the RAIL.

GUN PORTS. Most of the fighting vessel's guns were belowdecks and were fired through ports, which were always square and which were kept closed in dirty weather. A strange vessel's might show many gun ports but fail to have a gun behind each. On the other hand, the ports often were "masked"—that is, painted and perhaps planed to look like part of the side of the vessel, which because of this might be thought unarmed. The ports were opened from the inside, of course; and it was one of the tests of a good gun crew that it could get its port up and its gun run out almost simultaneously.

HALF-MOON. Another siege fortification, whether of earth or stone or some other material. It took its name from its shape, like the FLECHE.

HELM. The steering apparatus of a vessel, whether it was a jackstaff, a whipstaff, a tiller, or a wheel. To PUT UP ONE'S HELM was to turn sharply into the wind. It was the opposite of FALLING OFF, and it was a common trick when two vessels approached one another for purposes of fighting. Each sought to get the WEATHER GAGE.

HERMAPHRODITE. A brig with the mainmast fore-and-aft rigged like that of a schooner. It was popular with some sailors, who playfully called them "'morphodites," but it was not beloved by privateers.

HOLE, TO. To shoot a cannonball through the side of a ship, preferably "between wind and water"—that is, near the water line where it will do the most harm.

HOOK. A seaman's name for an anchor. These, by the way, never were "cast," as landlubbers like to have it. They were much too heavy for that. They were "dropped" or "let go."

HOT SHOT. Cannonballs heated red-hot before being fired.

HULL, TO. See HOLE, TO.

JIBS. The small, triangular sails in the forward part of a vessel, usually rigged between the foremast and the bowsprit. With other small sails, the SKYSAILS and the TOPGALLANTS and TOPSAILS, these comprised a warship's "fighting canvas." They were sufficient to keep way on the ship, so that she would answer her helm, yet they were small enough and remote enough so that they would not interfere with the working of the top deck guns if they were cut down by CHAIN SHOT or set afire by HOT SHOT.

JOLLY BOAT. A clincher-built ship's boat, smaller than a cutter, with a bluff bow and very wide transom, usually hoisted at the stern of the vessel and used chiefly as a hack-boat for small work.

JURY-RIG, TO. To make temporary, emergency repairs after a storm or a battle.

KEDGE, TO. To move a grounded vessel or one caught in a calm by means of a KEDGE ANCHOR, which is different from an ordinary anchor in that it is shaped not like a HOOK but like an opened umbrella. The KEDGE ANCHOR is carried some distance by a small boat, and dropped; and the vessel is worked painfully toward it by sailors WALKING THE CAPSTAN.

LAYER. That member of a gun crew who was assigned to "lay" the gun—that is, to raise or lower the muzzle—as distinguished from the man who actually aimed it. This was a very important post on a warship, and the rougher the weather the more important it was.

LINSTOCK. A rod about three feet long, with one end pointed so that it can be stuck upright into the deck, while the other end holds a MATCH, or piece of lighted fuse, by means of which the gun is actually fired. The word comes from two Dutch words meaning "match stick," which is just what it was. Though the flintlock for muskets was known as far back as the middle of the 16th Century, it was not until more than two centuries later that the principle was applied to cannons at sea. Most of even the later privateers used the LINSTOCK.

LONG BOAT. A vessel's largest smallboat. It might take as many as forty-odd men, and was used for towing, for cutting-out operations, etc., rather than for mere ship-to-shore errand running, for which the MOSES BOAT or the JOLLY BOAT would be preferred. The LONG BOAT often was equipped with a mast, and sometimes was decked over, or partly decked over. It was usually towed astern, being too big to haul aboard.

LONG TOM. A generic name for any long-barreled, long-ranging cannon, as distinguished from the stubbier CARRONADE.

MATCH TUB. A tub partly filled with water, in which was floated a piece of wood or of cork supporting a lighted fuse, called the MATCH. The LINSTOCK could be relit from this. There was usually one MATCH TUB to each gun, and it was an important part of the preparation for battle to see that these tubs were all out and in place—and lighted.

MOSES BOAT. A JOLLY BOAT. A small boat for ship-to-shore work. It was much used in the West Indies, but the name was common in New England too, and indeed the boat is said to have been named for Moses Lowell, a famous shipbuilder at Salisbury, Mass.

ORLOP. The lowest deck of a warship, just above the hold.

PIERCED. A vessel was said to have been PIERCED when her gunnels and part of her bulwarks had had GUN PORTS cut out of them. It was one of the first steps in converting a merchantman into a privateer.

POWDER MONKEY. A boy whose battle assignment it was to keep bringing gunpowder up from the magazines. Some of them were only 11 or 12 years old.

RAMMER. That member of a gun crew who rammed the powder home, then rammed the plug and the ball and the wad on top of it. Also, a RAMMER is the device with which he performs this task.

REDAN. A field fortification with the back open, much like a FLECHE.

ROPE-WALK. A long barnlike building in which rope for ships' rigging is manufactured and sold.

SEA ANCHOR. This is not an anchor at all in the ordinary sense of the word. It is a large square of canvas or tarpaulin with a rope tied to each corner, and it is thrown off the stern in a very bad blow. When it is not safe to spread any sail at all this serves to keep the vessel headed up into the wind.

SKYSAILS. The highest sails on a full-rigged ship, usually square, always high, spread just above the topgallants on the foremast and mainmast.

SPRINGS. Ropes or hawsers attached to the anchored cable of an anchored vessel. Sometimes these are for the purpose of preventing the vessel from swinging around and perhaps fouling another anchored vessel, and sometimes they were to make it easier to cut the anchor cable in case the vessel wished to get out of there in a hurry, leaving her anchors behind.

STUDDING SAILS. This is always pronounced and sometimes spelled STUNSAILS. They were fair-weather sails set out on spars on either side, temporary extensions of the fore and main booms, when the ship was driving right before the wind. They made for an ounce of extra speed. When a vessel had her STUDDING SAILS spread she was said to have "everything on but the cook's shirt."

SWABS. These were sometimes called SPONGES, and the man who used one was a SWABBER or a SPONGER. The instrument was like a broomstick with a long sponge mounted at one end. After a cannon had been fired the SWABBER dipped this into a bucket of water—there was always plenty of water standing around during a battle, for fear of fire—and then thrust it into the barrel of the gun, thus putting out every last little spark, an act that quite possibly saved the rammer's life. Firing made the barrel hot enough to evaporate the water almost as soon as it had done its job, so that the next charge of powder, put in with an instrument called a LADLE, was not wetted.

TEREDO, or TEREDOS. An animal about as big as your littlest fingernail. It fastens itself to the bottom of wooden ships in tropical waters, especially the West Indies, but unlike the barnacle it doesn't just hang on—it bores, it drills. Like the termite on land, the TEREDO within a few short months can make a good stout oak timber look like a wedge of Swiss cheese. It used to be called the TEREDO or TEREDOS *worm*, but we know now that it is not properly a worm but a mollusk.

TERREPLEIN. Originally the sloping ground on the inside of a fort's rampart, later the level land just below that, the place where the guns were mounted.

TOPGALLANTS. The sails mounted on the TOPGALLANT MASTS of full-rigged ships. This mast was the third one up, and the TOPGALLANT was just below the SKYSAIL.

TOPSAILS. Just below the TOPGALLANTS. The third sails down from the top.

TRUNNEL. Originally and properly TREENAIL. There was very little metal in the American colonies, or even in the American states just after the Revolution, and ships were customarily built and furniture made with wooden nails or pegs. These were TRUNNELS.

WALKING THE CAPSTAN (originally CAPSTERN). The CAPSTAN was a revolving pillar with a ratchet, turned by means of fitting-in bars that men pushed. This was the heaviest kind of work, such as kedging the vessel off a reef or fetching up the anchor.

WEATHER GAGE. The windward side of an enemy you were just about to tackle. Having the WEATHER GAGE was extremely important, as it allowed you to pick the time and angle of your attack, and whether in single vessel duels or big fleet actions hours and sometimes even days were spent in jockeying for this position.

WORMER. An iron double screw, sometimes on its own stick, sometimes mounted on the upper end of the SWAB or SPONGE. It was used from time to time after explosions to work out bits of old wadding or unburned scraps of the linen powder bag.

☆ BIBLIOGRAPHY

ADAMS, HENRY. *Historical Essays.* New York: Charles Scribner's Sons, 1891.

ADAMS, HENRY. *History of the United States during the Administrations of Thomas Jefferson and James Madison,* 4 volumes. New York: Albert and Charles Boni, 1930.

ALLEN, GARDNER WELD. *Massachusetts Privateers of the Revolution.* Boston: Massachusetts Historical Society, 1927.

ALLEN, GARDNER WELD. *Our Naval War with France.* Boston: Houghton Mifflin Company, 1909.

ANDREWS, CHARLES M. *The Colonial Period of American History* (volume 4: *England's Commercial and Colonial Policy*). New Haven: Yale University Press, 1938.

BEIRNE, FRANCIS F. *The War of 1812.* New York: E. P. Dutton & Company, 1949.

BOURNE, RUTH. *Queen Anne's Navy in the West Indies.* New Haven: Yale University Press, 1939.

BRADLES, FRANCIS B. C. *Blockade Running During the Civil War.* Salem, Mass.: The Essex Institute, 1925.

BRERETON, HENRY, see WATSON, MARRIOTT.

BURNEY, JAMES. *History of the Buccaneers of America.* New York: W. W. Norton & Company, Inc., 1950.

CARR, ALBERT Z. *The Coming of War: An Account of the Remarkable Events Leading to the War of 1812.* New York: Doubleday & Company, Inc. 1960.

171

CHAPELLE, HOWARD I. *The History of the American Sailing Navy: The Ships and Their Development.* New York: Bonanza Books, 1949.

CHAPIN, HOWARD M. *Privateering in King George's War, 1739–1748.* Providence, R.I.: W. E. Jackson & Co., 1928.

CHAPIN, HOWARD M. *Privateer Ships and Sailors: The First Century of American Colonial Privateering, 1615–1725.* Toulon (France): Imprimerie G. Mouton, 1926.

CHAPIN, HOWARD M. *Rhode Island Privateers in King George's War, 1739–1748.* Providence: The Rhode Island Historical Society, 1926.

CLARK, WILLIAM BELL. *George Washington's Navy.* Baton Rouge: Louisiana State University Press, 1960.

CRANWELL, JOHN PHILIPS, and CRANE, WILLIAM BOWERS. *Men of Marque: a History of Private Armed Vessels out of Baltimore, during the War of 1812.* New York: W. W. Norton & Company, 1940.

CRANWELL, JOHN PHILIPS. *The Log of the Rossie.* Maryland Historical Magazine, volume 35, No. 3, pp. 289–291; Baltimore, 1940.

CUTLER, CARL. *Greyhounds of the Sea: the Story of the American Clipper Ship.* New York: Halcyon House, 1930.

DALSEME, RENE. *Beaumarchais, 1732–1799,* translated from the French by Hannaford Bennett. New York: G. P. Putnam's Sons, 1929.

DECONDE, ALEXANDER. *Entangling Alliance: Politics and Diplomacy under George Washington.* Durham, N.C.: Duke University Press, 1958.

EASTMAN, RALPH M. *Some Famous Privateers of New England.* Boston: privately printed, 1928.

EMMONS, GEORGE F. *The Navy of the United States.* Washington: Gideon & Company, 1853.

FISH, STUYVESANT. *The New York Privateers, 1756–1763.* New York: George Grady Press, 1945.

FORESTER, C. S. *The Age of Fighting Sail.* Garden City, N.Y.: Doubleday & Company, 1956.

FREEMAN, DOUGLAS SOUTHALL. *George Washington: a Biography,* 6 volumes. New York: Charles Scribner's Sons, 1954 (vol. 6).

GOSSE, PHILIP. *The History of Piracy.* New York: Tudor Publishing Company, 1946.

HOLLIS, IRA N. *The Frigate Constitution: the Central Figure of the Navy under Sail.* Boston: Houghton Mifflin Company, 1900.

HUTCHINSON, J. R. *The Press-Gang, Afloat and Ashore.* New York: E. P. Dutton & Company, 1914.

JAMESON, JOHN FRANKLIN, editor. *Privateering and Piracy in the Colonial Period: Illustrative Documents.* New York: The Macmillan Company, 1923.

KARRAKER, CYRUS H. *Piracy Was a Business.* Rindge, N. H.: Richard R. Smith, Publishers, Inc., 1953.

KENDALL, CHARLES WYE. *Private Men-of-War.* London: P. Allan & Co., 1931.

KNOX, DUDLEY W. *The Naval Genius of George Washington.* Boston: Houghton Mifflin Company, 1932.

LIPPINCOTT, BERTRAM. *Indians, Privateers and High Society: A Rhode Island Sampler.* Philadelphia: J. B. Lippincott Company, 1961.

MACLAY, EDGAR STANTON. *A History of American Privateers.* New York: D. Appleton and Company, 1924.

MACLAY, EDGAR STANTON. *A History of the United States Navy from 1775 to 1894,* 3 volumes. New York: D. Appleton and Company, 1895.

MACMECHAN, ARCHIBALD. *Nova Scotia Privateers.* Toronto: The Ryerson Press, 1930.

MAHAN, ALFRED THAYER. *Sea Power in its Relations to the War of 1812.* Boston: Little, Brown and Company, 1910.

MAHAN, ALFRED THAYER. *The Influence of Sea Power upon the French Revolution and Empire,* 2 volumes. Boston: Little, Brown and Company, 1919.

MAHAN, ALFRED THAYER. *The Major Operations of the Navies*

in the War of American Independence. London: Sampson Low, Marston and Company, 1913.

McFee, William. *The Law of the Sea.* Philadelphia: J. B. Lippincott Company, 1950.

Minnegerode, Meade. *Jefferson, Friend of France: The Career of Edmond Charles Genêt.* New York: G. P. Putnam's Sons, 1928.

Morison, Samuel Eliot. *John Paul Jones: a Sailor's Biography.* Boston: Little, Brown and Company, 1959.

Mouzon, Harold A. *Privateers of Charleston in the War of 1812.* Charleston: Historical Commission of Charleston, 1954.

Munro, Wilfred Harold. *The Most Successful American Privateer: An Episode of the War of 1812.* Proceedings of the American Antiquarian Society, April 1913, pp. 12–62.

Paine, Ralph D. *Privateers of '76.* Philadelphia: The Penn Publishing Company, 1925.

Palmer, Benjamin F. *The Diary of Benjamin F. Palmer, Privateersman.* New Haven: The Tuttle, Morehouse, and Taylor Press, 1915.

Pares, Richard. *Colonial Blockade and Neutral Rights, 1739–1763.* Oxford: The Clarendon Press, 1938.

Peabody, Robert Ephraim. *The Log of the Grand Turk.* American Historical Review, volume 7, pp. 286–303.

Powell, J. W. Damer. *Bristol Privateers and Ships of War.* London: J. W. Arrowsmith, Ltd., 1930.

Robertson, E. Arnot. *The Spanish Town Papers.* London: The Cresset Press, 1959.

Robinson, William Morrison, Jr. *The Confederate Privateers.* New Haven: Yale University Press, 1928.

Roosevelt, Theodore. *The Naval War of 1812.* New York: Charles Scribner's Sons, 1926.

Russell, Phillips. *John Paul Jones, Man of Action.* New York: Brentano's, 1927.

Russell, Robert W. *A New Maritime Law: a Review of Mr.*

Marcy's Letter to M. de Sartiges. New York: W. C. Bryant and Company, 1856.

SHEFFIELD, W. P. *Privateermen of Newport.* Newport: John P. Sanborn, 1883.

SNIDER, CHARLES HENRY. *Under the Red Jack: Privateers of the Maritime Provinces of Canada in the War of 1812.* London: M. Hopkinson & Co., Ltd., 1928.

SPEARS, JOHN R. *The Story of the American Merchant Marine.* NY: The Macmillan Co., 1910.

STARK, FRANCIS R. *The Abolition of Privateering and the Declaration of Paris.* New York: Columbia University Press, 1897.

STATHAM, EDWARD PHILLIPS. *Privateers and Privateering.* New York: I. Pott and Company, 1910.

STRAUS, RALPH. *Lloyd's: The Gentlemen of the Coffee-House.* New York: Carrick & Evans, Inc., 1938.

THOMAS, CHARLES MARION. *American Neutrality in 1793: a Study in Cabinet Government.* New York: Columbia University Press, 1931.

TUNIS, EDWIN. *Oars, Sail and Steam.* New York and Cleveland: World Publishing Co., 1952.

WATSON, MARRIOTT, and BRERETON, HENRY. *The Privateers.* New York: Doubleday, Page and Company, 1907.

WHIPPLE, A. B. C. *Pirate: Rascals of the Spanish Main.* Garden City, N.Y.: Doubleday & Company, Inc., 1957.

WILBUR, MARGUERITE EYER. *The East India Company, and the British Empire in the Far East.* New York: Richard R. Smith, 1945.

☆ INDEX

177